VIDEO BASED
8 SESSION STUDY

FATHER'S
house

THE PATH THAT LEADS HOME

KAREN MCADAMS   RACHEL FAULKNER BROWN

Paperback: ISBN: 978-1-7361982-0-9

This workbook is a resource of Adventurously Expectant Life LLC

Printed in the United States of America

Edited by Rebecca Partain
Layout by Chel Kissler, Kreativity Inc.

Scripture quotations are from the Holy Bible. Translations and versions include: The Message, The Passion Translation, New American Standard Bible, New Living Translation, New International Version and New King James Version.

Cover art by Jensen Nemec

special thanks

We always say, "We are better together!" and each of you are living proof!

To Tricia Christian for her extraordinary writing contributions that are a testimony of what happens when you meet Grace in the person of Jesus Christ.

To Marie Tittle for believing that this could be "more," casting vision and collaborating with us.

To Ashley Williams for being our perpetual cheerleader and strategic samurai.

To Jensen Nemec for making magic from behind her camera lens.

To our *Be Still Prayer Team* ninjas who interceded constantly for you – the participants – to find your way home to Father's House.

To all of the past participants of Father's House, if it wasn't for you saying, "You've got to film this! This message has got to get out!", I'm pretty sure we would still be schlepping our binders, props and notes all over the state of Georgia.

To our families who supported us emotionally, financially and prayerfully through the process because you believe like we believe – that He is worthy of your time, talent and resources.

And finally and most importantly, to Jesus, Papa God and Holy Spirit who believed in us when we didn't quite believe in ourselves. YOU alone are the reason we can know beyond a shadow of a doubt that we truly belong in Father's House! YOU alone are the reason we want to get up and continue to shout the message of just how GOOD you truly are! We won't stop singing your praises until there's no air left in our lungs - YOU alone are worthy!

Hi there!

Karen McAdams

Encountering Abba Father and His relentless pursuit of my heart when I was so lost and broken changed everything for me. My greatest passion now is to see other women encounter our incredible Father and His powerful redeeming Grace.

Rachel Faulkner Brown

I love freedom more than anything else on earth and find myself saying at least once a day, "It is for FREEDOM that Christ has set us free." Walking out of the bondage of my secret unlocked a life I never knew was possible.

our promise

OVER THE COURSE OF
THE NEXT EIGHT WEEKS,
WE WANT TO JOIN YOU
ON THE JOURNEY HOME.
WE BELIEVE YOU WILL
DISCOVER THAT THERE
IS MORE FOR YOU THAN
YOU HAVE EVER DARED
TO DREAM!

table of contents

Hey friends!

Wow! We couldn't be more honored that you are joining us on this 8 week encounter-driven journey! To be sure, all of us are at different places in our journey. Between the two of us, we have been in enough ditches and hit enough potholes to know that none of us come through this life unscathed. But one thing we have learned is this: we are not alone! Jesus is right here with us, pointing the way home to our Father's House!

Over the course of the next 8 weeks, we want to join you as you embark on the path that leads Home. And guess what? We are fellow travelers with you! We certainly don't have it all figured out. But we want to open our lives to you and share some keys that we have discovered that have led us to find our seat at His table - all because we have discovered just how deeply loved and adored we are by the One we have come to call Papa God!

After taking hundreds of women through this course, we are certain of one thing: your life will not be the same on the other side! In fact, we believe that Papa, Jesus and Holy Spirit have drawn you to this very moment in time. Your breakthrough is just on the other side of the turning of these pages! We believe that in just eight short weeks, you will become what we call a "Go-To Girl" for the rest of your life all for His glory and for His beautiful renown!

We can't wait...see you on the path!

Karen + Rachel

HOW TO USE THIS
Study Guide

The Father's House Study Guide has been designed as a companion guide to the eight week Father's House video-based series. We believe that using this guide will greatly enrich your experience and help take your relationship with Papa God to a deeper, more intimate place.

Each session comes with:

Video Teaching
Each session is approximately 35 minute long.

Activation
An activation is a facilitated prayer time designed to help connect your head to your heart.

Listening Guide
The Listening Guide can be used to capture important points while watching the session video and to journal your experience during the Activation.

Daily reflections
Each week has 5 daily reflections that will take approximately 5-10 minutes to complete. Reflections include things such as crafted healing prayers, journal prompts, personal declarations, scripture reflections and our personal favorite... the letters from Papa God on Day 5.

Blueprint for Your Beliefs
Key scriptures from the content are provided in a variety of translations. We have intentionally used a number of translations to give your heart an opportunity to hear what perhaps has become overly familiar to you in a fresh new way. However, feel free to use whatever translation you are most comfortable with. Ideally you will want to meditate on one or two of these scriptures in the coming week, allowing them to engage you in a conversation with Holy Spirit. You may want to post these in a visible location as a daily reminder of what your Heavenly Father thinks about you!

Final thought...

Throughout the study, we have come to refer to Father God as Abba & Papa God. This simply reflects the heart change that we have gone through in how we now see Him. If you find this offensive, please substitute what feels more natural to you!

SELF ASSESSMENT
Questionnaire

Father God loves me as much as He loves Jesus.   TRUE / FALSE

Fellowship with Father God is broken until I confess and repent.   TRUE / FALSE

God answers my prayers on the basis of my obedience to Him.   TRUE / FALSE

I am as righteous as Jesus Christ.   TRUE / FALSE

I should work hard to live according to the Ten Commandments.   TRUE / FALSE

My righteousness before God is dependent on whether I am
living right before God.   TRUE / FALSE

The Holy Spirit's primary role is to convict me of sin.   TRUE / FALSE

Everything that Jesus said applies to my life.   TRUE / FALSE

My identity is a sinner who is saved by Grace.   TRUE / FALSE

God will sometimes cause accidents or sickness to test people or
grow them in their faith.   TRUE / FALSE

*Answer Key begins on page 147

FRIENDS & FAMILY
Commitment Letter

Dear _____,

You are so very important to me and so I'm asking for your support and encouragement as I take a journey over the next 8 weeks. I am participating in a study called Father's House. It is a journey to understand and experience that there is more for me than I knew. I am going to be expanding how I see myself, how I understand God's love for me and how I view what is possible for my life.

I'll be very focused over the next few weeks on leaning into some new beliefs and possibly undoing some lies that have limited my walk with the Lord. This study may forever change my life and the way I see Jesus, Father God and the Holy Spirit. But of course, this isn't just about me. As a fellow sojourner in my life, your support means the world to me. Thank you for praying for me, for allowing me to process with you and for supporting me on the path Home.

Love,

(Your Signature)

We have written this letter for you to share with your family and/or friends who know you are taking this study. This is an INVITATION for them to pray for you and partner with you in processing your journey. Please have them read this as you begin. We pray this letter brings connection, clarity and peace to you and the ones you love.

"I SAW MYSELF AS A LITTLE GIRL RUNNING TO FATHER'S HOUSE. AS I RAN, I GREW OLDER AND OLDER UNTIL I WAS MY CURRENT AGE. AS I ARRIVED AT THE HOUSE, HE WAS STANDING IN THE DOORWAY READY TO GREET ME WITH OPEN ARMS AND A BIG HUG. I FELT SUCH JOY AND PEACE TO BE FULLY ACCEPTED & LOVED BY MY FATHER."

♥ *Robyn*

SESSION ONE

The Journey Home

THIS RESURRECTION LIFE YOU
RECEIVED FROM GOD IS NOT A TIMID,
GRAVE-TENDING LIFE. IT'S
ADVENTUROUSLY EXPECTANT, GREETING
GOD WITH A CHILDLIKE "WHAT'S NEXT,
PAPA?" GOD'S SPIRIT TOUCHES OUR
SPIRITS AND CONFIRMS WHO WE
REALLY ARE. WE KNOW WHO HE IS, AND
WE KNOW WHO WE ARE: FATHER AND
CHILDREN. AND WE KNOW WE ARE
GOING TO GET WHAT'S COMING TO US -
AN UNBELIEVABLE INHERITANCE!

ROMANS 8:15-17 MSG

The journey starts here...

You are invited to come on a journey unlike any other. This journey will transform every aspect of life as you know it. It is the journey Home.

A journey, by definition, is the act of traveling from one place to another. The starting point for this sojourn is your "home" - the very life you are now living. What does your "home" look like? Its foundation is built on the beliefs, mindsets and behaviors you've cultivated all these years. You may feel really comfortable in the home you've created. The sounds are familiar and the smells are well known. Some cracks may appear in the foundation from time to time, but you know exactly how to cover them. Though, if truth were to be told, you find it hard to rest here. Repairs, renovations and upgrades are constantly needed to make your home measure up. The upkeep can be exhausting.

What if you could set the worries and responsibilities of tending to your home aside? What if you could pick up a yoke that is light and easy instead? The good news is the journey ahead requires nothing but a heart open to experiencing more - more freedom, more intimacy, more joy, more peace and more love.

Can you see up ahead? The path marked Home is littered with what's been released from daughters who are journeying with you. These are the masks torn off the faces who no longer must hide. These are the shoes taken off feet running the race of perfectionism. Here are the bottles of those finished self-medicating their pain. There is the make-up removed from the ones done with managing appearances, and here are the gloves thrown off hands giving up control.

Can you hear the singing? The voice of a daughter coming alive under the love and acceptance of her Papa is breathtaking. Did you catch a glimpse of her face? It's radiant with the joy of knowing who she is in her Papa's eyes.

Do you see Him? Papa is running towards you as He absolutely cannot wait for you to experience the extravagance of His love for you. His Home is built on the rock-solid foundation of the Gospel of His AMAZING GRACE. This gospel is rooted in three powerful truths: You are Lavishly Loved, Fully Forgiven and Radically Righteous. It is a foundation that never cracks... it stands the test of time!

Come and join your hands with ours as we journey together to Father's House. If you feel a little lost on the path, it's OK. You are never lost to Him. Your seat at His table is waiting. See the banner over Papa's front door? It simply reads, "It is finished." Together, let's discover exactly what was finished so you can live the adventurously expectant life your Father prepared for you!

Listening Guide

[KEY #1]

IT'S NOT ABOUT HOW GOOD I AM
BUT ABOUT HOW GOOD MY GOD IS.

Journal

Write down any impressions, pictures or feelings you experienced during the activation exercise. Ask Papa the following, "Papa, what are you saying to me?"

Daily Reflections

Day One

Please review your notes from this week's lesson. What is God highlighting for you?

_____

_____

_____

Up until now, how would you describe the journey that you have been on with the Lord?
What has the path looked like?

_____

_____

_____

How would you describe your family home (for example: nurturing, unpredictable, performance oriented)? What made you feel valued, worthy and loved?

_____

_____

_____

Karen and Rachel described the influence that their family of origin and denominations/religious teachings had on what they believed about God. The result was that they built their lives on a foundation of achieving, perfecting and trying to please God, rather than the foundation of God's amazing **GRACE**.

How would you describe the foundation that you have built your life upon?

_____

_____

_____

"Up until now" are key words for you because we believe that your life is about to change! If you could leave one thing behind and never pick it back up, what would it be?

For example: shame, performance, feeling unworthy, fear of failing, never feeling enough, etc.

_____

_____

_____

No matter what your journey has looked like *up until now*, in His home there is:

Freedom	Intimacy	Peace	Joy	Love	Rest
Vision	Purpose	Abundance	Health	Wholeness	Victory
Hope	Provision	Power	Worth	Confidence	Security

Circle the words that resonate most with your desires for this season or pick your own!

Write a prayer to your Father about your hopes for the next 8 weeks.

Dear Father God,

_____

_____

_____

_____

_____

While your new address is with Father in His house, your beliefs might have some catching up to do! Karen mentioned that her gospel wasn't exactly good news - it was a "Jesus plus" gospel. The result was that she was never quite sure whether all her efforts were truly enough. **Her mind had not been renewed to this week's key: "It's not about how good I am, but about how good God is."**

Imagine for a moment that you have decided to build a new home. The first thing the builder asks is for your blueprints. The blueprints determine the size of the foundation and ultimately how the house will be framed.

Guess what? Your beliefs are just like the blueprints! They determine the foundation you will build your life upon and "frame up" the life you will lead. Father's House is built on the **extravagant foundation of His amazing Grace**. A life lived in His house is a life of freedom, intimacy, peace and purpose! But here's the catch for most of us. We can't believe that He's actually that good and that this Grace is really that free, so we scale the foundation of our lives down to match our own small, narrow-minded beliefs! A life that is built on any other foundation than His Grace will never result in the abundant life that He longs for you to experience.

In your own words, how would you describe what the Gospel means to you?

_____

_____

_____

Read the passage below:
"For I am not ashamed of the Gospel (good news), because it is the *power* of God that brings *salvation* to everyone who *believes*." (Romans 1:16)

What an incredible passage of scripture. **HIS** power brings salvation when you do one thing - simply believe! Now that's what I call good news! But just what exactly does "salvation" encompass? Salvation is so much more than a one-way ticket to heaven or something that you only benefit from in the sweet by and by! Salvation is from the Greek root word "**sozo**".

SOZO means:

To Rescue	To heal (physically, mentally, emotionally, spiritually)
To Deliver	To make whole

The following passages use the word "saved" for the Greek word "sozo." Rewrite the following passages using your new definition. What do these passages tell you about what Jesus wants to do for you personally?

John 3:17

_____

_____

_____

Romans 10:13

_____

_____

_____

As a daughter in Father's House, we believe you were intended to experience the full "sozo." He wants you rescued, delivered into freedom, healed and made whole. In fact, this is what the abundant life is supposed to look like!

How does this belief challenge your current mindset? In what ways have you settled for "less than sozo"?

_____

_____

_____

Craft a prayer to Papa below for the areas of your life that you would like to see rescued, delivered, healed and made whole.

_____

_____

_____

_____

_____

_____

_____

_____

FOR OF HIS FULLNESS WE HAVE ALL RECEIVED GRACE UPON GRACE.

[JOHN 1:16 NASB]

What is Grace? Grace is the Greek word "Charis" and means unmerited favor, good will and loving-kindness. Favor means to lean towards, to share a benefit, extending and reaching for, to be gracious.

Grace is so much bigger than simply unmerited favor. These words paint a deeply moving portrait of who your Father God is and what this "Grace upon Grace" looks like. You could say that GRACE looks like Papa God leaning towards you and reaching out for you to give you a bear hug, tell you how much He delights in you and taking you by the hand to show you all the treasures He has for you in His house! The problem is that we have not always believed that He is just that good! Instead, we build our lives on trying to GET His hug, MERIT His delight and QUALIFY for His treasures.

You will need a new mindset - a goodness mindset - to be able to receive all the good things Papa God has for you. The Good News is that Holy Spirit and Jesus are here with you right now to help shift our perspective.

DOES THE GOD WHO LAVISHLY PROVIDES YOU WITH HIS OWN PRESENCE, HIS HOLY SPIRIT, WORKING THINGS IN YOUR LIVES YOU COULD NEVER DO FOR YOURSELVES, DOES HE DO THESE THINGS BECAUSE OF YOUR STRENUOUS MORAL STRIVING OR BECAUSE YOU TRUST HIM TO DO THEM IN YOU?

(GALATIANS 3:5 MSG)

Trust is like the key that unlocks the access to the treasure trove of "Grace upon Grace"- not striving, serving or even obeying! If **striving** lived at one end of the street and **trusting** lived at the other end, where would you say that you are? What/who do you specifically struggle to trust Him with?

_____

_____

_____

_____

In order to move from striving to trusting, you will need to frame your life with good beliefs. Let's ask Jesus, "What are you inviting me to believe about this 'Grace upon Grace'?"

_____

_____

_____

Papa God, thank you for what you are doing in your daughter's heart, mind and body. Thank you that you made receiving your Grace as simple as her trusting You, leaning in for a hug and opening her hands to let go in order to receive!

What would you like to express to Him today?

_____

_____

_____

_____

_____

_____

THE TONGUE HAS THE POWER OF LIFE AND DEATH IN IT...

[PROVERBS 18:21 NIV]

YOU WILL ALSO DECLARE A THING, AND IT WILL BE ESTABLISHED FOR YOU; SO LIGHT WILL SHINE ON YOUR WAYS.

[JOB 22:28 NKJV]

Sometimes you have to say something new to begin to truly believe something new! We use declarations as an amazing way of partnering with what Papa is already saying about you, your life and your future.

Create your own declarations for this week around Key #1. We will get you started, and then you can add to it:

It's not about how good I am but about how good my God is.

My Father is full of Grace, and He has good things planned for my life.

He's not good to me because I am good, He is good to me because He is good!

He understands where I am on my journey. I'm not behind; I am right on time.

I am open to receive from the fullness of His Grace. I am adventurously expectant.

While this might feel a little awkward to you, we want to encourage you to say these aloud each day! Your own tongue has been created by Papa to bring healing to your mind and your emotions. Let your body feel the beauty of this new Truth. In fact, neuroscience has shown us what God has known all along- that actually visualizing the truth you are declaring aloud, seeing and feeling the truth rather than just repeating it, creates new neural pathways to experience His truth as a living, experiential reality. If you sense some resistance, simply ask: What is the lie that I am believing that you want to uproot?

Dear daughter,

Will you take My hand and follow me? I can't wait to lead you Home. I've prepared a special place there just for you because My Home is not complete without you in it. From before the foundation of the world, I created you, my beloved one. I've counted every hair on your head and captured every tear you've ever cried. You are My beautiful daughter! Did you know that I couldn't be prouder to be your Father? I remember when you took your first steps! You were so full of excitement and anticipation. I was there cheering you on just as I am with you and for you now. As you wobbled and fell, I was there to catch you. Just as I will be there to catch your heart on this journey!

Just like I walked with Adam and Eve in the cool of the garden, my heart has always been to walk intimately with you. I long for you to know Me as I know you - to experience My glory and My extravagant love for you. Your heart is wired to connect with Me. Your ears are intricately designed to hear My voice. Trust the intentional way I've created every piece of you to relate to Me. Remain in Me, and I will remain in you. Never will there be a moment that I leave you or forsake you!

I know right where you are on your journey and the baggage that you have carried for so long. But it's time to begin unpacking those things - it's time to get unstuck! I will be with you every step of the way. In fact, I am the One who has brought you to this moment to give you a new perspective so that you can truly begin to see life through the lens of My perfect love. As you seek Me in the days to come, you will find My heart has always been turned towards you with a fierce and abiding love. There was never a moment that I turned from you. You will encounter Me if you will do just one thing... open your heart to Me. Will you take My hand my beloved daughter? Your journey Home has just begun.

Love,
Papa

Beliefs for My Blueprint

Underline or highlight any key phrases, allowing them to engage you in conversation with Holy Spirit. Is there a scripture that He is inviting you to meditate on this coming week?

—— ROMANS 8:15-17 MSG

This resurrection life you received from God is not a timid grave-tending life. It's adventurously expectant, greeting God with a child like, "What's next, Papa?" God's spirit touches our spirits and confirms who we really are. We know who He is, and we know who we are: Father and children.

—— JOHN 17:3 TPT

Eternal life means to know and experience you, as the only true God, and to know and experience Jesus Christ as the Son whom you have sent.

—— JOHN 10:10 NASB

The thief comes only to steal and kill and destroy; I came that you may have life, and have it abundantly.

—— JOHN 3:16-17 MSG

This is how much God loved the world: He gave His Son, His one and only Son. And this is why: so that no one need be destroyed; by believing in Him, anyone can have a whole and lasting life. God didn't go to all the trouble of sending His Son merely to point an accusing finger, telling the world how bad it was. He came to help, to put the world right again. Anyone who trusts in Him is acquitted; anyone who refuses to trust Him has long since been under the death sentence without knowing it. And why? Because of that person's failure to believe in the one-of-a-kind Son of God when introduced to Him.

—— 1 PETER 3:18 NLT

Christ suffered for our sins once for all time. He never sinned, but He died for sinners to bring you safely home to God.

NOTES

"I'M FINALLY ABLE TO HOLD ONTO THE FACT THAT I'M LAVISHLY LOVED VERSUS BEING TOLD MY ENTIRE LIFE THAT OBEDIENCE TO HIM COMES FIRST AND THEN HE WILL TAKE CARE OF ME. I SPENT MY ENTIRE LIFE TRYING TO BE THE GOOD GIRL. I HAVE BEEN ABLE TO SLOWLY OPEN UP AND BEGIN TO RECEIVE THE TRUTH THAT HE LOVES ME LAVISHLY, NO MATTER WHAT, AND I DON'T HAVE TO PERFORM OR 'DO THE RIGHT THINGS' FOR IT."

Lisa

SESSION TWO

Lavishly Loved

MOSTLY WHAT GOD DOES IS LOVE YOU. KEEP COMPANY WITH HIM AND LEARN A LIFE OF LOVE. OBSERVE HOW CHRIST LOVED US. HIS LOVE WAS NOT CAUTIOUS BUT EXTRAVAGANT. HE DIDN'T LOVE IN ORDER TO GET SOMETHING FROM US BUT TO GIVE EVERYTHING OF HIMSELF TO US. LOVE LIKE THAT.

EPHESIANS 5:1-2 MSG

The first tenet of the foundation

of Father's House is that you are Lavishly Loved. There is simply nothing you can do to make Him love you more and nothing you can do to make Him love you less. He loves you because He loves you because He loves you - He just can't help himself! Sometimes this can be easier for our minds to accept intellectually but much harder for our hearts to internalize and truly believe!

Why do you think that's so hard to believe? Well, the culture of this world reinforces a message that we are loved **if**... we accomplish, obey, perform, please, achieve, etc. Or, we are loved **because**... we have a certain characteristic, personality, appearance, trait, etc. Or, we are loved **until**... we disobey, disappoint, don't measure up, etc. Today's teaching focuses on the profound truth that has the power to completely transform the way you see yourself and the way God sees you forever:

IN FATHER'S HOUSE, YOU ARE SIMPLY LOVED, PERIOD!

Romans 5:8 (TPT) says, "But Christ proved God's passionate love for us by dying in our place while we were still lost and ungodly." The simple truth is that God chose you before you ever chose Him. He pursued you while you were still a hot mess. And He willingly sacrificed His son so you could freely receive His perfect love.

One of Jesus's final prayers to His Father before His arrest and crucifixion was recorded in John 17:26, "I have revealed you to them, and I will continue to do so. Then your love for me will be in them, and I will be in them. "Jesus prayed that the same love God has for Him will be in us! His prayer was answered when He spoke His final words on the cross, "It is finished"! (Luke 19:28). Your past? Finished. Your mistakes? Finished. Striving to measure up? Finished. Whatever you think would qualify His love... Finished!

Every condition of you being fully loved and accepted was accomplished by Jesus who now lives in you. Jesus's finished work on the cross tore down the veil separating you from His Father forever. When you accepted the free gift of His son as your Savior, you were given a new nature and new identity. In fact, what's true of Jesus is now true of you! Whenever God looks at you, He sees His beloved daughter. But if we stay locked into believing we are only loved **if**, we shackle ourselves to a life of striving, performing and achieving to earn His love. Jesus paid far too high a price for us to miss living in the radical freedom and joy of being loved without condition. No strings attached!

Just like we can only give what we have received, we can only live out what we believe. To live as a fully loved and accepted daughter in your Father's House, He's inviting you to let go of your former identity. You are no longer bound to your past, what anyone else has spoken over you or even what you say about yourself. As you journey Home, saturate yourself in who your Father says you are. He is **love**, and He is **Truth**. What He says about you is the truest thing about you. Friend, you are lavishly loved because... He said you are. His love for you is unchanging because He is unchanging. It's not too good to be true. It's the unfathomably good news of the Gospel. Believe it and receive it.

Listening Guide

$$\boxed{\text{KEY \#2}}$$

I BELIEVE THAT IT IS TRULY FINISHED.
I AM LAVISHLY LOVED AND COMPLETELY
ACCEPTED JUST AS I AM.

Father's House is built on the foundation of the Gospel of Grace - the Good News that you are:

- Lavishly Loved
- Fully Forgiven
- Radically Righteous

The journey is the _____ !
You are on a journey of discovering just how lavishly loved you are!

WE ARE BORN WITH 4 BASIC NEEDS;
LOVE, ACCEPTANCE, WORTH AND SECURITY.

In the 3 levels of brain development, you are trying to answer these questions:

- Am I safe?
- Am I _____ ?
- How can I learn from this?

Your **ifs** determine your core _____ and core fears.

How would you answer this question: People love me *if* _____

_____

_____

Therefore, I should _____

_____

_____

Three core truths:

He loves me...period! There are no IF's with the love of Father God. (Romans 5:8)

His love must be _____ . (Ephesians 5:2 MSG)

He loves you because He is _____ . (1 John 4:8)

Five things happen when you can say, "**Yes**, I am loved!"

You can receive a compliment with _____ .

You don't let the world determine your acceptance.

You recognize rejection can be _____ .

You look in the mirror differently.

You pursue others for _____ .

Jesus declared, "**IT** is Finished!" What is your **IT** that needs to be finished today?

_____

_____

_____

_____

_____

_____

_____

_____

_____

_____

_____

_____

_____

Journal

Write down any impressions, pictures or feelings you experienced during the activation exercise. Ask Papa the following, "Papa, what are you saying to me?"

Daily Reflections

> "LEARNING TO LIVE AS A LAVISHLY LOVED DAUGHTER IS A JOURNEY. EVEN THE MOST BATTLE-SCARRED HEART WILL MELT UNDER THE GAZE OF HIS PERFECT LOVE WHEN YOU SEE PAPA'S EXPRESSION WHEN HE LOOKS AT YOU."

Day One

Please review your notes from this week's lesson. What is God highlighting for you?

_____

_____

_____

Rachel said, "Father God loves you as much as He loves Jesus."
What does this statement mean to you personally?

_____

_____

_____

Perhaps you are feeling some resistance to this statement. What challenges do you encounter when accepting this Truth?

_____

_____

_____

_____

To know the Father's unconditional love requires that you also believe that He unconditionally accepts you just as you are. Spend some time with Father God and ask Him what He is inviting you to unconditionally accept about yourself that He already accepts about you?

_____

_____

_____

During the meditation, what was the "IF" you nailed to the cross?

      I am loved and accepted if _____.

      What happened when you nailed it to the cross?

_____

_____

Visualizing your future as a lavishly loved daughter is critical to your life. In fact, it helps engage your heart with your head when you involve your divine imagination. Describe what that life would look like in as much detail as possible. What would you be doing, thinking or feeling?

_____

_____

_____

_____

_____

_____

_____

_____

_____

_____

_____

_____

_____

This week we discussed that you may have picked up messages from your family of origin and life experiences that you are loved *if*. Did you know that we can put those messages on God as well?

Fill in the following:

Father God loves and accepts me *if* _____.

Father God loves and accepts me *if* _____.

How would you describe the impact these beliefs have had on your life and your relationship with Papa?

_____

_____

Today is a day to begin letting go of every *if* message you have been believing. It's a day to **trust Papa**, that with Him you are lavishly loved and completely accepted.

We want you to write a note to your younger self because she is pretty amazing! Consider this, do you need to thank her for how she has protected you or acknowledge the pain she has walked through? Maybe you want to celebrate her for the challenges she has overcome? Do you want to tell her how amazing she is? Let her know that from here forward, Papa's got this and He is inviting her to a life of being lavishly loved and completely accepted... just as she is!

_____

_____

_____

_____

_____

_____

_____

_____

Day Three

Mostly what God does is love you. Keep company with Him and learn a life of love.
Observe how Christ loved us. His love was not cautious but extravagant.
He didn't love to get something from us but to give everything of Himself to us.

[EPHESIANS 5:2 MSG]

NOW THAT'S WHAT I WOULD CALL LAVISH LOVE!

Lavish is a powerful word. It means superabundant and over the top, and it implies wasteful in extravagance. Father longs to lavish this kind of love upon you! But like Rachel said... we all need to work on being better "receivers." In fact, receiving is like the faucet that activates the flow of Grace in your life.

Today we are going to practice opening the faucet of your receiver!
You will need about 15 minutes for this exercise...

- Play "Lean Back" by Capital City Music.

- Prepare by taking a few cleansing breaths. Imagine inhaling the breath of Holy Spirit and exhaling cares and concerns.

- Picture what it would look and feel like to lean back into Papa's arms. Listen to His heartbeat. Feel the warmth coming from Him and the texture of His garment. Can you give yourself permission just to lean in a little closer than yesterday?

If you don't sense anything, it's OK! You can know that there is more for you, and He's fully committed to the journey of leading you into experiencing His lavish love. Learning to be a better receiver is a journey worthy of pursuit! Write about it below:

This week, ask Papa to show you how He lavishly loves and accepts you just as you are. Look for little "kisses" or God "winks" from Him, and journal those here.

Who in your sphere of influence could benefit from hearing about His lavish love and acceptance? Ask Papa to direct your next steps in communicating these Truths to those you've identified.

LETTING GO - These are powerful words for a daughter who is ready to move down the path and begin to live her life from a place of security and rest in Papa's House!

We all know that the enemy loves to lie to us. I think one of the areas he loves to lie to us the most has to do with just how much Papa loves us! The enemy loves to get us to hide behind masks. He loves to keep us on the hamster wheel of performing and self-improvement. He uses shame and rejection to speak his lies all in an attempt to get us to believe that we are loved and accepted *if*...

Let me ask you this, "Is there someone in your life who the enemy has used to get you to believe his lies?"

Forgiveness is the powerful tool that God uses to set you free from lies that have held you hostage. It is your ticket to disempowering these lies in your life! If you're willing, I believe that today is a great day to pursue your freedom.

Ask Father...

When did I first begin to believe the lie that I am loved and accepted *if*... (you may get a memory, event or age)

_____

_____

Is there someone I need to forgive for introducing this lie in my life?

Too often we bury or minimize our past hurts, but our heart still knows and holds a record - like a list of outstanding debts that someone owes you. We believe that it is incredibly helpful to identify the ways that this "cost" you. What was the cost or impact that this had on your life? Your relationships? your decisions?

_____

_____

_____

_____

Perhaps you would like to pray this prayer:

> Father, I choose to forgive _____ for the way that he/she reinforced the lie that I am only loved and accepted if _____.
>
> I choose to forgive him/her on the basis of your unconditional forgiveness for me first! If there is any debt I feel that they owe me, I cancel that debt. They owe me nothing!

Now visualize yourself handing Jesus the list of debts that your heart has been holding onto for so long. What does He do when you hand Him your list?

_____

_____

_____

Declare this: I renounce and break agreement with the lie that I am loved and accepted if...

_____

_____

_____

Jesus, what is the Truth you give me in exchange for this lie?

_____

_____

_____

MAKE WHAT HE JUST TOLD YOU
INTO YOUR DECLARATION FOR THIS WEEK!

Be sure to journal this experience - you won't want to forget what Papa has done for you!

_____

_____

_____

_____

_____

My dear daughter,

Slip off your shoes and sit at My feet. Rest in the sheer delight I have in simply being with you. Soak in My favor that takes great pride in who I've created you to be. Allow Me to hold up a mirror for a moment. What do you see? Your reflection has become so familiar to you. I see you scanning for every flaw. Breathe in My spirit of love. Exhale disappointment, disgust and discouragement. I declare peace to flow through every muscle of your body. I speak life into your eyes. I invite you to open them to see yourself the very same way that I see you.

If you could only see what I see... you were created in my image and possess staggering beauty yet the uniqueness of your beauty never ceases to take My breath away. You, My love, are My very favorite. I'm enamored by the sparkle in your eye, the curve of your face and the radiance of your presence. Did you know that you captivate Me? In all of time and space, there will never be another one of you. Let Me repeat that... there will never be another one of you! Why? Because I pulled out all the stops with you! I knit you together - every fiber of your body and being - with such exquisite care and love. I declare My work as **very good**. Hear My voice as I sing over you your very own love song. Allow the Truth of how I see you to penetrate deeply into your heart today.

I long for you to love yourself as I love you. For this is the greatest secret of all: as you allow Me to love you in abundance, you too will be able to love others. Out of the abundance of my acceptance, you too will be able to accept those who challenge you the most.

My kingdom is fueled by My love for you and your sisters and brothers. We call it perfect love because it's more than enough to answer the question on every child of mine's lips... "Am I enough?" As you receive My love you will become empowered to pour forth what you have received. Choose, My daughter, to simply receive what I give without measure... My perfect love!

Love,
Papa

Beliefs for My Blueprint

Underline or highlight any key phrases, allowing them to engage you in conversation with Holy Spirit. Is there a scripture that He is inviting you to meditate on this coming week?

—— ROMANS 5:8 TPT
But Christ proved God's passionate love for us by dying in our place while we were still lost and ungodly!

—— EPHESIANS 5:2 MSG
Mostly what God does is love you. Keep company with Him and learn a life of love. Observe how Christ loved us. His love is not cautious but extravagant. He didn't love in order to get something from us but to give everything of himself to us.

—— I JOHN 4:10-11 NIV
This is love: not that we loved God, but that He loved us and sent His Son as an atoning sacrifice for our sins. Dear friends, since God so loved us, we ought also to love one another.

—— ROMANS 8:15 TPT
And you did not receive the "spirit of religious duty," leading you back into the fear of never being good enough, but you have received the "Spirit of full acceptance" enfolding you into the family of God.

—— EPHESIAN 1:6 TPT
...for the same love He has for His Beloved One, Jesus, He has for us. And this unfolding plan brings Him great pleasure.

—— I JOHN 4:17-18 MSG
God is love. When we take up permanent residence in a life of love we live in God and God lives in us. This way, love has run of the house, becomes at home and mature in us, so that we're free of worry. On Judgement Day - our standing in the world is identical with Christ's. There is no room in love for fear. Well-formed love banishes fear...

"MY WHITE ROBE ISN'T DIRTY
ANYMORE. I PUT SHAME TO BED
FOR GOOD THIS MORNING!"

 Michelle

"MEMORIES OF MY OWN ABUSE
AND THE SHAME OF FEELING BROKEN
JUST LIFTED. FINALLY, I FEEL FREE!
I AM FREE OF THAT BONDAGE AND LIE
FOREVER. I AM GOING TO DANCE
WITH JESUS TODAY!"

Diana

Fully Forgiven

THERE IS NOTHING BETWEEN

YOU AND FATHER GOD, FOR HE

SEES YOU AS HOLY, FLAWLESS,

AND RESTORED!

COLOSSIANS 1:22 TPT

This week's lesson is all about learning how to walk in the freedom that comes to us when we receive the third key: you are fully forgiven forever! So many of us struggle with shame and condemnation for things we have done. Choices you have made in your past and secret regrets can hang like a heavy weight on your life. And then there's the painful words, betrayals or rejection that have a way of seeping deep down into your soul. You end up feeling stuck and unable to make traction in your journey to Father's House.

The good news is that you don't have to stay stuck. There is a way to leave behind the heavy baggage of shame and condemnation. This week, we invite you to let the blood of Jesus do all the heavy lifting. His final cry from the cross, "It is finished," was not for naught. Do you need forgiveness? He cast your sin away "as far as the east is from the west." Do you need healing? His death and resurrection made it possible for every wounded part of your soul to be free and whole.

One of the most profound characteristics of Jesus is the way He dealt with sinners - you know, the ones that the religious people of His day discarded and scorned. Consider His encounter with the Samaritan woman who was married no less than 5 times and was now living with her sixth beau. She clearly had not lived a life that would earn her gold stars at the big white church down the street. Yet, this is the woman Jesus chose to reveal, for the fist time recorded in scripture, that He was in fact the long awaited Messiah. This is the sinful woman whom Jesus chose to offer His living water.

What's the significance of this offer of living water? Living water is a term for the running water that was used to declare a person ceremonially clean, such as in preparation for a wedding ceremony or entry into the priesthood. When Jesus offered her living water, He was really saying, "Beloved daughter, I make what the world calls 'unworthy' into beautiful brides. I turn prostitutes into priests. I change stained garments into white robes!!" And, through His work on the cross, He says the same to you.

If we could imagine what transpired during that encounter between Jesus and the Samaritan woman, we might see the moment that she looked into Jesus's eyes and found what her soul had always been looking for yet never knew it needed. She had tried to fill the wound in her soul for so long. All it did was bring her more pain, more rejection and more unbearable shame. And then, she encountered the love of Jesus. In Him, she found lasting forgiveness that washed her white as snow and empowered her to be one of the greatest female evangelists of her time.

When you receive what Jesus freely gives, things change. You change! Sadly, far too few of us are living as though we are forgiven period. You'll know there is still more freedom for you if you're not resting in total confidence that Father God sees you as completely innocent - as though you had never sinned!

What would change if you believed that everything that was required to make you fully loved and fully forgiven in your Father's eyes was fully accomplished in the finished work of the cross? You might just find the next time you mess up, you don't need to hide your face. You can run straight into your Father's arms where He'll pick you up and remind you who you are and how fully forgiven you already are! Redemption never looked so beautiful as it does on a woman who has lived mired in shame and discovers the scandalous good news that declares her fully forgiven forever!

Listening Guide

[KEY #3]

I AM FULLY FORGIVEN... FOREVER.

Three places where beliefs about sin/forgiveness come from:
- Your _____
- House of God
- Word of God

How did these contribute to your beliefs about sin, Father God's response to you, and how you received forgiveness?

_____

_____

_____

WHAT DOES "REPENTANCE" MEAN TO YOU?

Repentance simply means to change _____ mind.

In the story of original sin in the Garden of Eden (Genesis 3), how do you see the story unfolding - particularly in regard to the 3 questions God asks:

- Where are you?
- Who told you that you were naked?
- What is this that you have done?

Sin doesn't change how God sees you...sin changes how **YOU** see you!

Religion says: Repent first, **then** God.
Grace says: You are forgiven _____.

"You were dead because of your sins and because your sinful nature was not yet cut away. Then God made you alive with Christ, for He forgave **all** our sins. He canceled the record of the charges against us and took it away by nailing it to the cross. In this way, He disarmed the spiritual rulers and authorities. He shamed them publicly by His victory over them on the cross." [Colossians 2:13-15 NLT]

Three things were **Finished** at the cross:

    1. Your old sin nature
       He didn't just die for you - He died as _____.

    2. The sin slate
       The only one reminding you of your sins are you and the enemy.

    3. The power of your _____!

It's not that you are just forgiven... it's that you are _____.
This is your new redeemed identity!

Journal

Write down any impressions, pictures or feelings you experienced during the activation exercise. Ask Papa the following, "Papa, what are you saying to me?"

Daily Reflections

SHAME AND INTIMACY WILL NEVER SHARE A SEAT AT THE SAME TABLE. YOU HAVE TO LET GO OF ONE TO HAVE THE OTHER. FORGIVENESS ERASES THE RECORD OF SHAME AND SAYS, "COME TAKE YOUR SEAT NEXT TO PAPA!"

Day One

Please review your notes from this week's lesson. What is God highlighting for you?

_____

_____

_____

What challenges did you encounter as you heard today's message?

_____

_____

_____

How did your home life, the church or other influences shape your views of forgiveness and Father's response to your failures?

_____

_____

_____

What are 1 or 2 new beliefs that Father God is inviting you to lean into this week?

_____

_____

_____

Consider this statement: "Father God doesn't just consider you forgiven, but He sees you as completely innocent - as though you had never sinned." What are your thoughts?

_____

_____

_____

Day Two

FORGIVENESS

Knowing this, that our old man was crucified with Him, that the body of sin might be done away with, that we should no longer be slaves of sin. **For he who has died has been freed from sin**... Likewise you also, reckon yourselves to be dead indeed to sin, but alive to God in Christ Jesus our Lord.
[ROMANS 6:6, 11 NKJV]

So what do we do? Keep on sinning so God can keep on forgiving? I should hope not! If we've left the country where sin is sovereign **how can we still live in our old house there**? Or didn't you realize we packed up and left there for good? That is what happened in baptism. When we went under the water, we left the old country of sin behind, when we came up out of the water, we entered into the new country of GRACE - a new life in a new land!
[ROMANS 6:1-3 MSG]

One degree... that's all it takes for a ship to end up in an entirely different destination. Well, the same can be said for your beliefs. One small shift in your beliefs has the powerful potential to change your most important relationship - your relationship with your Heavenly Father. Let's talk about some of those beliefs.

Most of us have heard that God's love for us is unconditional, and hopefully by now you are beginning to let that Truth take root in your heart. However, if I asked you if His forgiveness is unconditional, would you be as confident?

We believe that many women are living as "Friday" Christians.

- A Friday Christian is a woman who is still stuck in her past, confessing the same sins over and over... never really living in the freedom and innocence that Friday purchased for her!

- A Friday Christian is a woman who is more focused on staying forgiven than believing she is forgiven.

- A Friday Christian believes her own actions are more powerful than Jesus's actions.

To a Friday Christian Jesus might have said **IT** is finished, but in her mind, it's really not finished. Have you ever noticed with what stunning detail that you can recall some of the things on your sin slate but you can't remember what you had for dinner last night?

In order for us to move out of Friday and into resurrection Sunday, we are going to need to let Father God do some translation work for us on some terms that get a lot of airtime in Christian circles: confession and repentance. We will look at confession today and repentance tomorrow.

In your own words please define the word *Confess*.

Let's see how close your definition aligns. According to HELPS Word Studies and Strongs Concordance **confess** is defined as:

To voice the same conclusion (HELPS)
To agree, to speak the same (Strongs)

(If you're anything like me, that's a little different than how I approached the word "confess." I thought it meant "to make a list of all my sins!")

NOW, LET'S CONSIDER CONFESSION UNDER THE OLD COVENANT VERSUS THE NEW COVENANT.

Under the Old Covenant, confession centered around an elaborate sin management system with blood sacrifices. There was only one major problem with that system – your conscience was never clean and you were forgiven "until." The only thing you were truly confident in was this: your forgiveness was contingent on **YOU** - Your performance, your obedience and finding your spotless sacrifice. The only conclusion the sinner could draw was that, well, he was still a sinner! The blood of bulls and goats could neither cleanse his conscience nor change his identity - he was still a sinner.

Please read what the New Covenant says in Colossians 2:13-14, Ephesians 1:4-8 and Hebrews 10:11-23. What do these passages say to you personally about your sins and your new identity?

Under the New Covenant, absolutely everything changed. You were forgiven **before** you sinned, not **until** you sinned. When it comes to sin, Father God wants you to "confess" or "voice the same conclusion" and "agree, speak the same" as what He says about you... you are holy and blameless before His unconditional love which includes unconditional forgiveness! Daughter, He's made up his mind about you and you are not powerful enough to change it. Just ask the Samaritan woman!

So are we saying you shouldn't talk to God about sin and personal failures? Absolutely not! There's nothing quite like getting things off your chest. In fact, talking to Papa God about your failures and struggles is both absolutely liberating and healing to your soul. But here's the thing – the New Covenant approach is completely different. You don't do it to **get** forgiven but because you **are** forgiven.

SO WHAT SHOULD YOU DO WHEN YOU SIN?

Run! Run straight into Father's arms! Under Grace, you get to respond to His lavish love by running to Papa with your failures and acknowledge how your sin hurt you and hurt His heart as well. But guess what? Rather than Him giving you a stern, disappointed glare, you get to listen to Him respond with a simple, "I know what you've done, beloved. But that's not who you are anymore! Let me tell you who you really are... in fact, let me tell you about Sunday!"

Remember under Grace, **IT IS FINISHED** is your starting point! At the cross, **ALL** of your sins were paid for – even the ones you can't remember or haven't even committed yet. This is not a hall pass on sin – this is just the goodness of a Gospel that our human mind struggles to comprehend!

A NEW COVENANT CONFESSION

While Old Covenant confession centered around sin, New Covenant confession centers around Christ. What does Romans 10:9 say about confession?

To be sure, central to our faith is confessing that you have sinned and fallen short of the glory of God. It's the famous confession of 1 John 1:9 that if we confess (say the same thing as Him) that we have sinned, He will cleanse us from all unrighteousness. But we don't stop there – that would be living in Friday. Our next confession is Jesus!! Jesus who is the answer to our "fallen short" problem!

Here's the almost too good to be true news: The old you – the sinner carrying her sin slate – died [Romans 6:6]. When Christ was raised from the dead, so were you! You were not just forgiven, you were raised innocent. Daughter, you were made free, blameless and a new creation in Christ. When you believe what Father God believes about you, you will move right into Sunday's powerful declaration - you are fully forgiven forever!

Journal your thoughts on today's reflection below:

_____

_____

_____

Day Three
REPENTANCE

Isn't this amazing news... this almost too good to be true Good News? In the new covenant of Grace, unconditional love also has unconditional forgiveness for you. And **love** Himself has declared **It is finished**. All of your sins were paid for before you even showed up on planet earth. But, like everything with this new covenant, it's all about **receiving by faith** this **Grace** in which we now stand!

Today we want to look at your definition of the word *Repentance*.

How do you define repentance?

_____

Perhaps you have believed, like us, that repentance has its focus on you and your actions. You believe that by you listing your sins, committing to God that you have heartily amended your ways, and making a heartfelt pledge to never return to your old ways will change His mind towards you. How's that working out for you? Religion will always put you in the driver's seat. It tells you that there is something **you** must do in order to get **God** to do something for you. Did you know that's actually a holdover from the Old Covenant?

Old Covenant repentance focused on **what** you were turning away **from** (sin), but New Covenant repentance focuses on **who** you are turning **to** (Jesus).

According to Strong's concordance, repentance is the Greek work "metanoia" and simply means:

To change one's mind

And "meta" from the word "metanoia" means:

Changed after being with

You see, if you hang out in Father's House long enough, you can't help but change your mind because of WHO you are WITH. And your behavior will follow what you believe!

If you believe you are a sinner, you will constantly work on your behavior. Like the prodigal son, you will offer to work in Father's fields (or serve at church or tithe more or never yell at your kids again) because you can't imagine that there's really nothing you need to do to prove your repentance is genuine. You may even believe your professional apology will change your Father's mind. What's amazing about this story is that before the son could read his professional apology, mow the grass or even harvest the fields, he's already been loved on, cleaned up and invited inside for an intimate celebration by his father! Whose mind do you think was changed (or would we say completely blown)?

How does Father God get us to Repent?
Read Romans 2:4. Write your own interpretation below.

_____

_____

How have you seen His kindness in your life, and how has this changed your mind?

_____

_____

Read Luke 5:5-11. What does this story say to you about the power of God's kindness?

_____

So what does Grace-based repentance look like for us on this side of the cross? It's Father God taking you to Friday's cross and re-"minding" you that it's His kindness towards you that took all your sins, nailed them to the cross and marked them *paid in full*. It's Him re-"minding" you that there are no slates in His House. Here's the thing... since Jesus is the Door (John 10:9) to Father's House, you can choose to either live on the front porch with your slate or you can enter through Christ, your perfect sacrifice. It's completely up to you!

And in Father's House, you will find life revolves around a different kind of work - Jesus, Father and Holy Spirit (the dream team) assuring you of your new identity and how you are lavishly loved and fully forgiven. They know that when you live from this kind of love and acceptance, in this *no condemnation* lifestyle, things change! You change! The shame and insecurity that formerly held you completely loses its grip. You will find that there's no room anymore for secrets in your life - life is just too short, right? You will find yourself actually excited about your life and the destiny that God has planned for you, dreaming with Papa about the amazing adventures He has for you as His beloved daughter.

What are 1-2 beliefs that you think Papa is inviting you to change your mind (repent) about?

_____

_____

_____

_____

_____

_____

For contemplation, play Natalie Grant's song "Clean." Picture your past, present and future sin slate being nailed to the cross. **Journal your experience below.**

_____

_____

_____

_____

_____

_____

_____

_____

_____

_____

_____

_____

SO NOW THE CASE IS CLOSED. THERE REMAINS NO ACCUSING
VOICE OF CONDEMNATION AGAINST THOSE WHO ARE JOINED
IN LIFE-UNION WITH JESUS, THE ANOINTED ONE.
[ROMANS 8:1]

IT is truly finished! In other words, anything the enemy would use against you to accuse you or con-demn you, was nailed to the cross. Have you received what He has provided, or are you still beating yourself up over things from your past?

_____

_____

The enemy would love to make you think **IT** is not finished. He specializes in reminding you of your past - of the things that have been done by you or to you. He torments you with your secrets. Isn't it time you stopped putting up with him? There are too many exciting things in your future to be ruled by your past!

Let's process some of this so that you can move forward. (You may want to position yourself in a quiet spot with no distractions for this exercise.)

Ask Papa the following: Is there a specific memory you want to talk to me about that is causing me to stay stuck in condemnation? Briefly describe it below.

_____

_____

_____

We invite you to pray this prayer:

Jesus, I come to you with this memory that's been toxic in my life and has weighed me down with guilt and condemnation. (Be patient here. Lean into what you are sensing He is bringing up.)

Jesus, can you show me where you were at this time?

_____

Jesus, what have I been believing as a result of this toxic memory?

_____

Jesus, what is the Truth?

_____

Pray the following:

Jesus, I choose to let this go into your hands. (You may want to see yourself giving this memory to Jesus. Watch Him take it, and see what He does.)

Jesus, today, I want to receive your forgiveness for the things that I have done. (See yourself receiving this washing by His living water. What do you notice?)

Jesus, I choose to release forgiveness to _____ for participating in hurting me. Jesus, will you wash my mind, will, emotions and any place in my body that has hosted this toxic memory with your cleansing blood. Please touch and heal every broken place in my heart and bring me freedom and wholeness in its place.

Jesus, what do you give me in exchange for this toxic memory? (Write down what you hear or see.)

_____

_____

_____

Jesus, what is a new declaration that you want me to begin declaring about myself?

_____

_____

Thank you for loving me, forgiving me and healing me today!
Note: You can use this prayer framework in the days to come as it's really just a conversation starter to bring you into deeper freedom and abundance!

Sweet girl,

Sit a moment, and let Me tenderly hold you. I need you to carefully listen to Me today. I need you to know that you were and are never alone. I wiped every single tear from your eyes and wept alongside you as the pain, the pressure and the brokenness became too much. Let Me gently remove the weight of guilt and shame. It's not for you to carry anymore. I love you far too much to let you stay in this place of regret and remorse.

I sent My precious Son to bear the weight of your sin and shame so you could live free - free to experience the depth of My love for you with no barriers. So, my girl, come sit with Me. Rest in My loving kindness. Put down your fear of condemnation so that you make room for your heart to pick up confident expectation in Me. Expect that I always create beauty from ashes. Expect that I'm not focused on sin, rather, I'm focused on calling you up to your identity as My beautiful daughter.

Do you know why My Son has so perfectly taken care of sin? He has done it so that it is no longer a stumbling block that prevents you from running straight to Me even when you fail or falter! Shame might stand like a bully on your path, but I am training you in the ways of freedom! You live in a no condemnation zone, so you can run that shame bully over when he tries to bully you! As you come alive to who I am in you and for you, you will stop focusing on all the ways you see what's wrong with you.

Did you know that when I look at you, I don't see what's wrong with you? I only see what's missing in your walk with Me. And I'm totally committed to empowering you to experience My goodness. As My presence grows in you, so will your expectation of the goodness you'll receive. Rest in My favor so you can drench others with the overflow!

Love,
Papa

Beliefs for My Blueprint

Underline or highlight any key phrases, allowing them to engage you in conversation with Holy Spirit. Is there a scripture that He is inviting you to meditate on this coming week?

—— COLOSSIANS 1:22 TPT
There is nothing between you and Father God, for He sees you as holy, flawless, and restored.

—— COLOSSIANS 2:14 TPT
He canceled out every legal violation we had on our record and the old arrest warrant that stood to indict us. He erased it all - our sins, our stained soul - He deleted it all and they cannot be retrieved! Everything we once were in Adam has been placed onto His cross and nailed permanently there as a public display of cancellation.

——ROMANS 6:6-11 MSG
Could it be any clearer? Our old way of life was nailed to the cross with Christ, a decisive end to that sin - miserable life - no longer captive to sin's demands! ... From now on, think of it this way - sin speaks a dead language that means nothing to you; God speaks your mother tongue, and you hang on every word. You are dead to sin and alive to God. That's what Jesus did.

—— HEBREWS 10:17 NKJV
And then He adds, "Their sins and lawless deeds I will remember no more."

—— ROMANS 8:1-2 NIV
Therefore, there is now no condemnation for those who are in Christ Jesus, because through Christ Jesus the law of the Spirit who gives life has set you free from the law of sin and death.

—— PSALM 103:3 TPT
You kissed my heart with forgiveness in spite of all I've done.

—— EPHESIANS 1:4 TPT
And He chose us to be His very own, joining us to Himself even before He laid the foundation of the universe! Because of His great love, He ordained us so that we would be seen as holy in His eyes with an unstained innocence.

NOTES

"I'VE BEEN A CHRISTIAN SINCE I
WAS 8 YEARS OLD AND I'VE NEVER
HEARD THIS. WHILE I BELIEVED I
WAS FORGIVEN, I WAS NEVER ONE
OF THOSE RIGHTEOUS CHRISTIANS.
I'M BEGINNING TO BELIEVE THIS IS
TRUE OF ME TOO."

♥ Tara

Radically Righteous

OUR FAITH IN JESUS NOW TRANSFERS
GOD'S RIGHTEOUSNESS TO US AND
HE NOW DECLARES US FLAWLESS IN
HIS EYES. THIS MEANS WE CAN NOW
ENJOY TRUE AND LASTING PEACE
WITH GOD, ALL BECAUSE OF WHAT
OUR LORD JESUS, THE ANOINTED
ONE, HAS DONE FOR US.

ROMANS 5:1 TPT

How are you doing...

on this journey of actually believing you belong in your Father's House? Some of you may feel a sense of excitement and an awakening in your spirit while others of you may feel like you've been hit by a truck and can't get your bearings. Wherever you are is exactly where you should be! Remember, the journey IS the destination. Breathe deeply and know that the presence of Christ is in you and with you every step of the way!

This session is focused on the third element of the foundation of Father's House: you are radically righteous. For most of us, the shift in believing we don't have to "do right" to "become right" is almost impossible to accept. Even though we are told over and over that Grace is a free gift of faith, we do everything in our power to earn it and prove to God we deserve it. We scream, "Doesn't my obedience count?"

The thing is that no amount of doing, striving, proving, performing or earning will ever be enough to accomplish what Jesus has already done. When you placed your faith in Christ, your identity changed forever.

The fascinating truth is that the old you, the you that is still trying to measure up, died. You see, Christ didn't just die for you. He died as you. In other words, everything that was unrighteous about your old nature died! And when He was raised, you were raised with Him - in His prefect righteousness.

Galatians 2:20 TPT says it clearly: "My old identity has been co-crucified with Messiah and **no longer lives**; for the nails of His cross crucified me with Him. And now the essence of this new life is no longer mine, for the Anointed One lives His life through me - we live in union as one!" And, Romans 6:6 continues, "Could it be any clearer that our former identity is now and forever deprived of its power!"

The glorious good news is that you, my friend, have been brought into the perfect righteousness of God when you "do" one thing and one thing only: simply believe. Your new identity is declared flawless in His eyes. But what so many of us do is run right back to the grave where our old selves were buried and continuously try to perform cosmetic surgery on a version of ourselves that is completely dead. We literally attempt to pretty up our corpse with a little lipstick, some blush and new clothes to present ourselves "worthy" instead of believing and receiving that what Jesus did on the cross was more than enough to make us fully acceptable to our Father.

What would your life look like if you threw the towel in on all that self-effort? What if instead of striving you simply rested and received what He has freely given to you - the robe of His perfect righteousness? Let's simply do the work of believing that He really is that good and walk confidently in our position as His righteous daughter.

Listening Guide

[KEY #4]

I AM AS RIGHTEOUS AS JESUS CHRIST.

Righteousness means to be in a condition _____ to God, to be innocent, holy and just.

The problem arises when we treat righteousness like a *verb* - like something we *do* to *become*.

Righteousness is about what *Jesus* has done _____ to make you _____ with Father God!

Righteousness is simply received, not achieved.

What if the question is not what must **I DO** but rather, what must **I BELIEVE**?

Three empowering *Grace beliefs* about your righteousness:

Righteousness is not dependent on your _____ .
Romans 5:19

_____

_____

_____

Given as a _____ .
2 Corinthians 5:21

"You stand before God as if you were Christ because Christ stood before God as if He were you." - Charles Spurgeon

_____

_____

_____

Received by _____ , not by feeling.
Romans 5:1

_____

_____

_____

How do we walk this out: Rest and Renew! (Ephesians 4:23-24)

We put *off* our old self and put on our *new* self - created in true righteousness!

Righteousness fully _____ you for:

Provision - (Proverbs 10:6, Psalm 5:12)

Protection - (Psalm 34:17)

Power to Reign - (Romans 5:17)

When *you* believe what *He* believes about you, 3 things happen:

Effortless _____ .

Enter into His _____ .

Tap into your heart's desires!

Journal

Write down any impressions, pictures or feelings you experienced during the activation exercise. Ask Papa the following, "Papa, what are you saying to me?"

Daily Reflections

Day One

Please review your notes from this week's lesson. What is God highlighting for you?

_____

_____

_____

Up until now, where were you on the "righteousness" scale? _____ (1-10)

What holds you back from believing you are as righteous as Jesus Christ?

_____

_____

_____

_____

_____

_____

_____

"You were taught, with regard to your former way of life, to put off your old self, which is being corrupted by its deceitful desires; to be made new in the attitude of your minds; and to put on the new self, created to be like God in true righteousness and holiness."

Jesus is holding out the robe of righteousness to you. He wants you to "enduo" it - put it on and sink down into it like the most amazing robe you have ever put on - only better! Take some time to picture this as your new reality - it is like your second skin! He gives you this picture so that you can remember what He already knows to be true of you!

What specific beliefs would help align your thinking with this Truth?

If you are trying to be the perfect mom, wife or Christian, you may not always get it "right," but you can rest in knowing that you are "right" in Father's sight!

Read the following

"When He has come, He will convict the world of sin, of righteousness, and of judgment. Of sin, because they do not believe in me; of righteousness because I go to my Father and you see me no more; and of judgment because the ruler of this world is judged."
(John 16:8 NKJV)

Did you know that this is the only time in the entire New Testament that there is mention of Holy Spirit convicting of sin? And as we can see here it is in response to those who do not believe in Him! Wow!

As a believer, this says He wants to convict you of something completely different: your righteousness. Why not sin? Because sin was dealt with at the Cross thoroughly for all time! Heaven works on a different standard than earth. Holy Spirit knows that reminding you of who you are, the righteousness of God in Christ, empowers you to say "no" to sin and "yes" to Christ-centered living.

Let's consider the word "convict." The word convict can mean to "convince or bring to light." What does it mean to you that the Holy Spirit wants to convince you and bring to light your righteousness rather than your past sins?

When do you think Holy Spirit is most likely to tell you that you are righteous? When you mess up or have it all together? What feelings or actions does that provoke in you?

Today, let's write a note to your Father thanking Him for your new robe of righteousness. It's OK if you are still struggling to believe that you don't have to "do right things" to be right with Him or to get the right response from Him. Simply share your thoughts with Him and listen for His response.

Day Three

Read Luke 15:11-32 in your favorite translation.

Boy, can I ever relate to the Son with His nose to the grindstone working hard in the fields! I would definitely have been the one screaming, "It's not fair! Don't you see how hard I am working for you, how obedient I am - how good I am at following all of the good Christian girl rules? I tithe, I bring gifts to the needy at Christmas and I read my Bible every morning!! I deserve to be blessed!"

I can hear Papa's response to me, "Daughter, I am so crazy about you. Did you know that as my daughter, you are not my day laborer or even my servant? As my daughter, you can have anything of mine - it's yours! There's just one thing that I ask of you... you must be willing to simply receive it on the basis of my goodness... not yours!"

In what ways can you personally relate to the two sons in the story?

The story is actually quite tragic because only one son found His seat at the table that day - the son who believed that His Papa was just that good, just that kind and just that gracious.

Consider this: the Gospel of Grace is a love story to some and a tragedy to others. To those who want to work and perform their way into a seat at the table, it will end in tragedy. But to those who believe it's a story of perfect love, well let's just say, it ends with a lavish wedding and a Bride!

What will it be for you? Papa God is so good that He offers you His very own robe of perfect righteousness, but He will not force you to take it. It must be received by you through faith alone - simply trusting that He is just that good!

When you wear this robe, even when you mess up or fail to serve Him perfectly, you are still perfectly right with Papa God! Why? Because it is not your righteousness that you are wearing - it is His. When you sink into this robe, it redefines your life. It literally swallows up all that you were so that you become all that He is - perfect righteousness!

Do you need to take something off before you put it on? How do you feel when you put it on? Now step over the threshold and see Papa's response to your arrival. What are you thinking or feeling?

Write about it below...

Read Romans 5:17. What are the two keys to reigning in life?

Create your own righteousness declaration based on the following:

I am as righteous as Jesus even when I (am not perfect, unkind, impatient, selfish, etc.)

_____

_____

Because I am righteous, Papa loves to _____ .

_____

I don't have to _____ in order to be right with Papa.

I am right with Papa because of what Jesus has done right!

Precious girl,

Isn't it time that you retired the running shoes from the exhausting treadmill of performance? I know it's hard for you to believe, but sweet one, you never had to earn through your performance what has already been freely given by your position in My Home. It was secured when My Son went all the way for you... all the way to the Cross! Did you know that We still remember it daily? The robes of righteousness My children wear are a daily reminder to all of us in My realm of just how successful our Cross truly was.

You have been trying to take the servant's entrance for far too long. I know it has felt familiar to you but we want to introduce you to a new way of living and being. We know that your love spurs you on to want to do amazing things for Me, but first you must learn to take your seat of rest. It is only then that you are ready to run the race that I have for you. Otherwise you will be tempted to earn what has already been freely given.

Remember the day you placed your faith in Me? Oh, My Beloved, I do. All of heaven threw a party in celebration of your adoption. You were forever grafted into My family. On that day, and forevermore, I clothed you in the righteousness of My Son. From head to toe, I transformed you. Your old identity died with My Son, and when He rose, you rose in glory with Him. You are now seated in the heavenlies clothed in the righteousness of My Son!

I'm delighted how you are discovering what, up until now, you have only dared to believe! I would love to hear what's on your heart! What if you dared to believe that your desires actually originated in Me? I have amazing plans for you... plans that will astound you! It's so exciting for Me to watch as you discover the amazing provision of My favor and blessings. But even more so, My heart beams to see you learning to reign with dignity and Grace over the enemy of your soul. I'm not surprised at what a quick learner you truly are! Remember... every day... to put on your robe. Sink into it! Renew your mind to this Truth: you are as righteous as your elder brother Jesus, and that makes you an inheritor alongside Him in My Heavenly realms.

Love, *Papa*

Beliefs for My Blueprint

What key phrases is Abba highlighting to you in the passages below? Underline or highlight them.

—— ROMANS 5:1-2 TPT
Our faith in Jesus transfers God's righteousness to us and He now declares us flawless in His eyes. This means we can now enjoy true and lasting peace with God, all because of what our Lord Jesus, the Anointed One, has done for us. Our faith guarantees us permanent access into this marvelous kindness that has given us a perfect relationship with God. What incredible joy bursts forth within us as we keep on celebrating our hope of experiencing God's glory!

—— ROMANS 5:15-16 TPT
Now, there is no comparison between Adam's transgression and the gracious gift that we experience. For the gift far outweighs the crime. It's true that many died because of one man's transgression, but how much greater will God's Grace and His gracious gift of acceptance overflow to many because of what one Man, Jesus, the Messiah, did for us! And this free - flowing gift imparts to us much more than what was given to us through the one who sinned. For because of one transgression we are all facing a death sentence with a verdict of "Guilty!" But this gracious gift leaves us free from our many failures and brings us into the perfect righteousness of God - acquitted with the words "Not guilty!"

——2 CORINTHIANS 5:21 NKJV
For He made Him who knew no sin to be sin for us, that we might become the righteousness of God in Him.

—— GALATIONS 3:5-6 MSG
Answer this question: Does the God who lavishly provides you with His own presence, His Holy Spirit, working things in your life you could never do for yourselves, does He do these things because of your strenuous moral striving or because you trust Him to do then in you? Don't these things happen among you just as they happened with Abraham? He believed God, and that act of belief was turned into a life that was right with God.

—— ROMANS 5:17 NIV
For if by the trespass of the one man, death reigned through that one man, how much more will those who receive God's abundant provision of grace and of the gift of righteousness reign in life through the one man, Jesus Christ.

NOTES

"MY FIRST 'EXPERIENCE' WITH HIM, DURING ONE OF THE ACTIVATIONS, WAS IN MY OLD HOUSE. IT WAS POWERFUL! SO POWERFUL I TRIED TO REVISIT THE OLD HOUSE AGAIN, HOPING HE WOULD SPEAK TO ME EVEN MORE. HE DID MEET ME THERE THE SECOND TIME, BUT ONLY TO TELL ME THERE WAS NOTHING MORE TO DO HERE. THEN HE WALKED ME TO HIS HOUSE AND BROUGHT ME TO MY NEW ROOM! IMMEDIATELY I WAS ASKING 'OK, WHAT'S NEXT? WHAT DO YOU HAVE FOR ME TO DO HERE?' HE SAID 'REST'. REST!"

Naomi

Freedom in the House

CHRIST HAS SET US FREE TO

LIVE A FREE LIFE. SO, TAKE

YOUR STAND! NEVER AGAIN LET

ANYONE PUT A HARNESS OF

SLAVERY ON YOU!

———————

GALATIANS 5:1 MSG

Sweet friend, we hope you are starting to taste and see that your Father is not just good, He is altogether amazing in every single way. Our prayer is that you are starting to experience the staggering lengths that Jesus and Abba Daddy went to in order to lavishly love you, fully forgive you and make you radically righteous.

But the good news doesn't stop there. The key we will be unlocking in this week's session is that you are free to experience every good thing from your Father. Jesus's death didn't just set you free *from* sin and shame, it set you free *to* experience freedom and the pouring out of His inheritance for you. It's far better than anything that could come in a beautiful blue Tiffany's box!

This begs the question, freedom from what? You may be very familiar with the Ten Commandments and the many laws in the Old Testament you've been taught to obey. Those laws are referred to as the Old Covenant - an agreement God made with the nation of Israel before Christ. Those laws were God's standard of what was holy and just. There was just one major problem. Try as you might, following those laws lacked the power to make you holy and just before God.

Enter Jesus who came not to abolish the Law, but to fulfill it. When Jesus hung on the cross and said, "It is Finished," He drew a line in the sand declaring an end to the old Covenant and ushered in a new, better way. He called it a New Covenant! This covenant would not be established on rules but rather on a relationship. In other words, if you have ever tried memorizing the Ten Commandments, now might be a good time to give up on that endeavor!

Why was a new way necessary? Let's go back to the heart of our Father. He created us in His image so we could experience an intimate relationship with Him. He didn't create us to be hired helpers who robotically obey Him because we have to or should. At the cross, Jesus purchased our freedom from a rule-based relationship so you could be adopted as His child. This profound act of love was an invitation for you to become a daughter empowered by the limitless gifts of His love.

However, it can be really challenging to break our rule-based habits. Ironically, one of the biggest obstacles to relating to God as our Abba Daddy is how we read and interpret God's word. Before you think we're missing the mark, allow us to illustrate this concept. Have you ever put on a set of glasses with the wrong prescription? If you have, you know the uncomfortable feeling of seeing everything with blurred vision. The prescription may be just right for someone else and give them crystal clear sight but causes you headaches and a lack of clarity and perspective.

The same is true for us if we apply an Old Covenant lens of "what do I have to *do* to earn God's love and favor" to the gospel of Grace. As daughters in our Father's House, we need to put on the correct glasses whenever we read His word - glasses that filter every verse through the New Covenant lens of "what has Jesus already *done*" through the finished work of the cross! Reading the Bible with a recognition of *who* was being spoken to, *when* and for *what* purpose frees us to recognize what applies to us as daughters living under the New Covenant versus what was applicable and spoken to the nation of Israel living under the Old Covenant.

Jesus's death and resurrection was the ultimate invitation to run and play in your Father's House as the beloved daughter that you are. The only rule He has for you is to simply believe and receive the freedom He paid such a high price for you to experience - freedom to be led by the Spirit, live a life without limitation and lean into the glorious riches of His inheritance.

Additional Thoughts

At this point in the study, you may feel like we've taken a wrecking ball to the house where you once lived so comfortably - the house where the rules hung on the wall and your slate was carefully managed and kept clean! As the old blueprint of beliefs is deconstructed, we want to encourage you to keep pressing in!

Holy Spirit promises that He will lead you into all Truth, and when you know the Truth, it will set you free. We believe that when you rightly divide the Word, you will find Truth that leads to freedom on every page of scripture. So how do we rightly divide the Word that leads us to Truth? We begin with recognizing a few key points...

ALL SCRIPTURE IS TRUE - IT JUST MAY NOT ALL APPLY TO YOU.

Sounds like heresy, doesn't it? But, it really is true! Let us show you why. The Bible is actually a book of covenants (or agreements) between God and either nations or people. Some of these covenants apply to you and some do not! For example, God made a covenant with Noah to never flood the earth again. You and I are still benefiting from that covenant. On the other hand, the Old Covenant that God made with the nation of Israel does not apply to you!

We get tripped up when we assume that because it is the 'Word of God' every word written on its pages applies to us. Not so fast. It all depends on which covenant the writer is referring to.

For our purposes, we want to hone in on 2 main covenants: the Old Covenant (aka Mosaic Covenant/ Law) and the New Covenant.

Let's look at some of the differences between the Old and the New Covenant.

OLD COVENANT	NEW COVENANT
Between God and Israel	Between God and Jesus
Conditional Covenant	Unconditional Covenant
Performance-based	Grace-based
Ten Commandments/613 Laws	Laws of Love, Liberty and Life in the Spirit
Duration: Mt. Sinai to the Cross	Duration: Cross to Eternity

When you put your faith in Christ, you became a participant in the New Covenant. Hebrews tells us that this New Covenant is a **better** covenant founded on **better** promises! Better than what? Better than the Old Covenant! What made it better? Well for starters, it was not based on a list of rules to be performed but a relationship to be enjoyed!

Where the confusion comes in is where we read the Old Testament, specifically the Old Covenant, and try to apply it all to our lives just because it is "the Word of God." But Jesus and Father God only relate to you based on the Covenant that you are in, and that is the New Covenant based on His matchless Grace and mercy!

So does that mean you should stop reading the Old Testament? Of course not! In fact, we are incredibly encouraged as we read about the prophetic pictures of Jesus's coming and of the New Covenant that He would make with all of humanity - a covenant that would reconcile us back to the heart of His Papa and bring us into an intimate relationship!

Let's check out what some Old Testament prophets have to say about this new covenant that was coming in. Please read Ezekiel 36:26, Jeremiah 31:31-34 and Isaiah 54:9-10.

WHAT MIGHT BE SOME NEW OBSERVATIONS FOR YOU?

- The Old Covenant was never your covenant unless you lived a very, very long time ago and were part of the nation of Israel.

- Following the rules/Laws of the Old Covenant (obeying the 10 commandments) never made anyone holy and just before God, including Israel. (Romans 3:19-21)

- If you like to hang onto your Ten Commandments, consider this: the Law only has two applications for you - to convict people of unrighteousness (Romans 7:7) and to lead you to the One who could make you righteous, Christ himself. (Galatians 3:24)

- When Jesus said, "It is finished," He was nailing all of the conditions of the Law to the cross! In the New Covenant, there are no qualifications or conditions to experience Papa's love, acceptance and forgiveness. That's why it's called Grace! He's just that good.

- The New Covenant did not BEGIN at Matthew 1 - it began at the END of the Gospels, at Jesus's death, burial and resurrection! (Luke 22:20)

The Gospels reflect a period of transition from Law to Grace, Old to New, Duty to Delight. Jesus ministered to those living under the Law. He elevated the Law to the self-righteous. Why? To raise the bar beyond their reach! But for sinners, He elevated the Love and Grace of His Papa. Why two different approaches? Because both approaches were intended to take them to the same door - the door that would give them access to Papa's House!

Going forward...what might be helpful for you when reading scripture?

Ask: What covenant does this passage apply to?
Discern: Does this covenant apply to me?
Pray: Jesus, what do you want to reveal to me from this passage?

OLD COVENANT	NEW COVENANT
God	Abba
Servant	Daughter
Striving	Resting
Achieving	Believing
Sins Covered	Sin Removed
Spiritual Death	Eternal Life
Do	Done
Self Righteousness	God's Righteousness
Rules	Relationship
Generational Curses	Inheritance

Listening Guide

$$\left[\; \text{KEY \#5} \;\right]$$

I BELIEVE I AM FREE TO RECEIVE EVERY GOOD THING FROM MY FATHER.

The Bible is made up of 5 main covenants: Noahic, Abrahamic, Davidic, Mosaic and the New Covenant.

Mosaic Covenant = Old Covenant = the _____

> Ten Commandments plus 613 other Laws.
> It was an "**If, then**" system - **If** you obey, **then** you will be blessed.

> The Law is holy, just and good, but it is _____ to make you holy, just and good. The problem was not the Law... we were the problem!

Why did God give the Law? Two reasons:

> To clearly reveal _____ and the sin nature of mankind.
> (Romans 7:7)

> To end self _____ and lead them to Christ.
> (Galatians 3:24)

The Dilemma: Our sin nature

> We come into this world with a spirit that is **not** alive to God - unable to love God with all your heart, soul and mind.

The Solution: Jesus

Jesus is the _____ to our dilemma! He fulfilled the **Law** perfectly for all of humanity forever! (Matthew 5:17)

The Gospels are a period of _____ between the Law and Grace. Jesus elevates the Law to the self-righteous, He extends Grace to the unrighteous.

What are the New Covenant "Laws"? Love, Liberty and the Spirit of Life in Christ!

What do you get as a daughter of the New Covenant?

L - Led by the Spirit
L - Live a Life without Limits
L - Lean into your inheritance

Jesus paid the price... your inheritance is _____ !
Are you receiving what HE gave you?

Journal

Write down any impressions, pictures or feelings you experienced during the activation exercise. Ask Papa the following, "Papa, what are you saying to me?"

Daily Reflections

THE ONLY RULE IN FATHER'S HOUSE IS
"FOLLOW ME AND BELIEVE LIKE A LITTLE CHILD."

Day One

Please review your notes from this week's lesson. What is God highlighting for you?

_____

_____

_____

What challenges did you encounter as you heard today's message?

_____

_____

_____

What are your thoughts about this statement: "Everything in the Bible is true - it just doesn't all apply to you." Can you give an example of how this might be accurate?

_____

_____

_____

_____

Does it change how you read the Gospels when you reflect on this statement: "Jesus was speaking to people who were still under the Old Covenant. He was elevating the Law to the self-righteous and elevating grace to sinners."

Do you think you can "fall from Grace"? Read Galatians 5:1-4. What does Paul say? What does that say to you?

Read 2 Corinthians 3:7-18. What observations do you make about the Old Covenant vs. the New Covenant?

Day Two

For no matter how many promises God has made, they are yes in Christ.
And so through Him the "Amen" is spoken by us to the glory of God.

[2 CORINTHIANS 1:20 NIV]

One of the glorious aspects of the New Covenant is that every promise is "yes" because of our new position in Christ.

Listed below are just a few of the promises you have access to as a daughter in the New Covenant. Underline which ones you want to receive by faith for your life.

- No weapon formed against me can prosper. (Isaiah 54:17)
- I am innocent, holy and blameless before Father. (Colossians 1:22)
- I reign in life with authority and power. (Romans 5:17, Luke 10:19)
- God is my refuge and strength. He is my great defender. (Psalm 46:1, Psalm 18:2)
- I do not have to fear. Papa is for me! Who can stand against me? (2 Timothy 1:7)
- Father God, Jesus and Holy Spirit are causing all things to work together for
  my good. (Romans 8:28)
- I can trust God to finish what He began in my life as I abide in Him. (Philippians 1:6)
- By His stripes, I am healed physically, emotionally, mentally and spiritually. (Isaiah 53:5)
- I have the peace of God - I am in continual fellowship with Papa. (Romans 5:1)
- I enjoy an abundant, overflowing life. (John 10:10)
- God is always on my side, and I am more than a conqueror through Christ Jesus. (Romans 8:31, 37)

What would you like to add?

_____

_____

Mark 11:25 says, "Whatever you ask for in prayer, believe that you have received it and it shall be yours." Why do you think "believing that you have already received it" is important to Papa?

_____

_____

_____

Take one of your promises above and imagine you already have it. In as much detail as possible, write what your life looks like.

_____

_____

_____

What steps can you take to place these promises front and center in your daily routine?

_____

_____

_____

Day Three

Read Galatians 3:13-14 and Deuteronomy 28.

Jesus is all-around good news for your life! At the cross, Jesus not only paid the penalty for your sin, but He also fully absorbed every "curse" for you. What is a "curse"? It is simply the opposite of a blessing. It's an area where you see a family pattern of chronic sickness or disease such as diabetes, cancer, heart disease, lack, poverty, breakdown of family, dementia, addiction and generational mental health issues.

Here's the glorious news - because of what Jesus **finished**, what ran in your family line ran out at the cross! You see, Jesus didn't just die for your sins, He died to take **every** curse too! Hear me now sister, **no** curse can stand against the blood of Jesus!

Consider your own family tree...
What destructive family patterns run in your family line?

_____

_____

_____

_____

Are there any similarities to Deuteronomy 28? We've got wonderful news! You have been grafted into a new family tree - the Tree of Life and Life More Abundant! He took on **your** family tree so that you could take on **His** family tree. What does this inspire inside of you?

Pray this prayer:

Jesus, Thank you so much that you went above and beyond what I ever dreamed. Thank you for dying on the cross for my sins!

Thank you that you didn't stop there. You took all my family patterns of _____ into your body and declared, "**It is finished**!"

I am agreeing with you today, Jesus! I declare that, "**It is finished**" also! I place the blood of Jesus and the cross of Christ in between my family tree and me.

I declare that my family lives in the avalanche of generational blessings instead.

I declare to my family line that you are blessed to walk in divine health, peace, abundance, mental stability and prosperity of body, soul and spirit.

By faith, I receive the fullness of what you did on the cross for my family and for me.

In Jesus name, "**It is finished!**"

What does your future look like as you contemplate your new family tree? Is there a picture, a scripture or a song that comes to mind?

_____

_____

_____

_____

_____

_____

_____

_____

_____

_____

_____

On Day Two you discovered some amazing promises that Father God has made to you!

How can you personalize those promises and turn them into your very own declarations? We also want you to add a new step to your declarations - see or visualize those promises making their way out of heaven and into your life. Wendy Backlund says, "Faith is not blind - it is actually visionary!" We couldn't agree more! Happy declaring!

Day Five

My baby girl,

I can sense your anxious thoughts. I see your mind racing about the future. Slow down and breathe. Exhale fear and inhale My peace. I am singing My promises over your soul. Let them wash over you and fill your mind and body with confidence. My promises are true for you. When you face challenges and obstacles, anchor yourself in the hope and assurance of My Truth. I am putting opportunities in your life to grow your trust and faith in me. How do I do this? By giving you endless encounters with My goodness. My promises are a guarantee of who I am and who I will be for you at this moment.

The prize of My promises is a relationship with Me. So, beautiful one, abide in Me. When you stay in Me, it is impossible for My promises to not be fulfilled. I cannot go back on My word. In me, you are free to believe what I have spoken to you and to receive what I have for you. Listen to Me in the stillness. In the quietness of you heart, I will speak. When doubt creeps in, keep your eyes on Me. Don't look to the left or to the right. Proclaim what I have promised and practice the language of possibility! You're learning to be content using a new muscle - the muscle of rest and trust. Don't give up, My precious... I assure you, the dividends are so worth it!

As you wait on My response with a carefree heart, trust that My plans are perfect. My timing is just right. I am holding you in My perfect embrace.

All My Love,
Abba Daddy

Beliefs for My Blueprint

What key phrases are Abba highlighting to you in the passages below? Underline or highlight them.

—— GALATIANS 3:13-14 MSG
Christ redeemed us from that self-defeating, cursed life by absorbing it completely into Himself. Do you remember the Scripture that says, "Cursed is everyone who hangs on a tree"? That is what happened when Jesus was nailed to the cross: He became a curse, and at the same time dissolved the curse. And now, because of that, the air is cleared and we can see that Abraham's blessing is present and available...

—— GALATIANS 3:23-25 NIV
Before the coming of this faith, we were held in custody under the Law, locked up until the faith that was to come would be revealed. So the Law was our guardian until Christ came that we might be justified by faith. Now that this faith has come, we are no longer under a guardian (the Law).

——GALATIANS 5:1 MSG
Christ has set us free to live a free life. So take your stand! Never again let anyone put a harness of slavery on you!

—— JEREMIAH 32:40 NKJV
And I will make an everlasting covenant with them, that I will not turn away from doing them good; but I will put My fear in their hearts so that they will not depart from Me.

—— 2 CORINTHIANS 1:20 MSG
Whatever God has promised gets stamped with the Yes of Jesus.

—— ISAIAH 54:9-10 NIV
To me this is like the days of Noah, when I swore the waters of Noah would never again cover the earth. So now I have sworn not to be angry with you, never to rebuke you again. Though the mountains be shaken and the hills be removed, yet my unfailing love for you will not be shaken nor my covenant of peace be removed, says the Lord who has compassion on you.

"I HAVE FALLEN ASLEEP FOR THE LAST FEW NIGHTS PRAYING WITH MY HAND OVER MY HEART DECLARING MY IDENTITY AND WHOLENESS. THE LORD BROUGHT ME CLARITY OF A TIME IN MY LIFE WHERE LIES OF NOT BEING WORTHY, CHOSEN AND UGLY TOOK HOLD. I FELT HIM SAYING TO ME, 'NO MORE HIDING. YOUR DESIRE TO BE BEAUTIFUL, LOVELY AND WORTHY IS ALREADY TRUE.'"

♥ *Laura*

SESSION SIX
Who I Am

... BECAUSE ALL THAT

JESUS NOW IS, SO ARE

WE IN THIS WORLD.

———————

1 JOHN 4:17 TPT

Have you ever experienced identity theft?

It can leave you feeling incredibly vulnerable, helpless, angry and afraid. There is nothing more exposing and terrifying than having the core of who you are stripped away in an invisible attack. Yet, as believers, it happens to every single one of us. The enemy's most potent tool to stop us from living in the power, freedom and authority we have as our Father's daughters is to steal, kill and destroy our identity.

The enemy knows that what you believe about yourself dictates how you think, feel, act, react and ultimately, who you become. In the Kingdom, who you are releases what you do. The enemy tries to convince you WHAT you do determines WHO you are. That's why Satan attacks what you believe about yourselves the hardest. You're not alone in being targeted. When Jesus first entered His years of ministry, John baptized Him. "And a voice came from heaven, this is my beloved Son in whom I am well pleased" (Mark 1:11 NKJV). Jesus was then led by the Spirit into the wilderness where He was tempted by the devil. What did he test Him on first and foremost? His identity.

"*If* you are the Son of God, tell these stones to become bread..."
"*If* you are the Son of God, throw yourself down..."

Have you ever noticed that the enemy left out one key word? He left out "beloved."

Jesus is the perfect role model for you when the enemy comes to challenge your identity! He replied with the Truth of God's word. We have the great opportunity and privilege to do the same. The enemy is the father of all lies. He speaks His native language of lies which births condemnation, oppression, depression and discouragement. He has not been, or will ever be, like your Father. That's why we need to wake up and tend to the areas of our hearts and lives that so desperately need our Father's love and Truth.

The degree to which we are convinced in our hearts of our new identity and can rest in the security of that is the degree to which we will experience the reality of it in our inner lives. We'll be able to live from the inside out with our spirit leading our soul rather than our soul leading the charge!

Did you know that an amazing thing happened at your new birth? You became just like the Son. In the same way that He and Papa live as One, now you live as One. The implications of this are staggering and will take an eternity to truly unpack.

He grafted you into the very being of your Father. You have been written into the palm of His hand. You have been adopted as His delightful child, and the same love He has for Jesus, He has for you. You are not second best or His second choice. He paid the ultimate price in sacrificing His son to bring YOU home to Papa. That is why we have the Spirit in us that cries out Abba Father.

What if you began to live from the position of pure confidence, security and rootedness that you indeed belong to your Father? What He says about you is the truest thing about you: you are chosen, dead to sin, a new creation, seated in power and authority and His very masterpiece!

Listening Guide

[KEY #6]

WHATEVER IS TRUE OF JESUS IS TRUE OF ME!

...because as He is, so are we in this world. (1 John 4:17)

"The identity of _____ you are releases **what** you do." - Leif Hetland

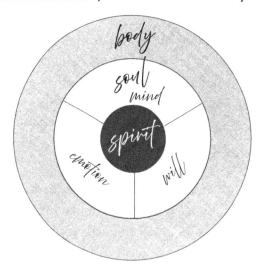

You are a spirit being, who has a _____, living in a body.
(1 Thessalonians 5:23)

Spirit - One with God
Soul - Mind, Will, Emotions
Body - Physical body

You were intended to live Spirit ⟶ informs Soul ⟶ Body & World

A "soul takeover" happens when we are living out of our _____, ruled by our soul instead of our spirit!

What are the "open apps" in your soul?

> These are the things from our past that are still running the show of our life, draining our energy, and determining our reactions and choices rather than the NEW life of the Spirit inside of us!

What words would you use to describe Jesus?

As He *is*, so are you! In your *spirit*, you actually already are all of those things!

What is one word He is inviting you to begin believing today?

If He is _____ , then I am _____ .

Five fingerprints of your identity:

> You are _____ . (I Peter 2:9-10)
>
> You are _____ to sin as an identity!! You are not "a sinner!"
> (Romans 6:11)
>
> You are a new creation. (2 Corinthians 5:17)
>
> You are seated in power and _____ . (Ephesians 2:6)
>
> You are a masterpiece. (Ephesians 2:10)

The power has been generated, and I am being invited to "flip the switch" on the resurrection power and authority that has been deposited into my spirit!

When you know who you are:

> You can say, I am Papa's _____ !
>
> You bring others up!
>
> You don't live in _____ !
>
> The world dims!
>
> You walk in freedom!

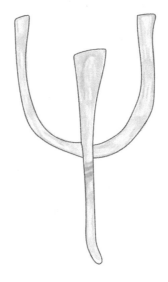

The Hebrew language is both pictographic and alpha-numeric. The Hebrew Letter also called "**Hey**" corresponds to the number 5 which stands for **Grace**. When God added the "**Hey**" to Abram's name, He was placing His Grace upon His life... just like He does for you!

His **Grace** upon your life makes what is impossible become _____ !

Journal

Write down any impressions, pictures or feelings you experienced during the activation exercise. Ask Papa the following, "Papa, what are you saying to me?"

Daily Reflections

Day One

Please review your session notes. What is Father God highlighting for you?

_____

_____

_____

In what ways have you seen your *soul* ruling through the "open apps" of your past? (Rachel called this a "soul takeover.")

_____

_____

_____

How does knowing that your *spirit* wants to influence your *soul* change the way you see yourself?

_____

_____

_____

Your spirit has already been made perfect, but your *soul* may need some renovation work. What are some "I am" statements that have plagued your mind?

_____

_____

_____

Read Romans 12:2. How does Holy Spirit want to partner with you for a Romans 12:2 transformation?

_____

_____

_____

If whatever is true of Jesus is true of you, what does that say about you?

If Jesus is _____ , then I am _____ .

If Jesus is _____ , then I am _____ .

If Jesus is _____ , then I am _____ .

*Day Two*

What you believe the Father believes when He looks at you is probably one of your most important beliefs. In fact, who you are is meant to tell the world who Jesus is because whatever is true of Him is true of you! He is the blueprint for your new identity!

But did you know that the enemy is downright threatened that you are going to discover what he already knows to be true? He knows that you are a masterpiece and Papa's favorite. He knows you have an amazing destiny and that you're filled with incredible gifts that lie dormant inside of you like buried treasure. The question is, do you?

When King David was still a shepherd boy, he penned these amazing words.

"How precious to me are your thoughts, God! How vast is the sum of them! Were I to count them, they would outnumber the grains of sand." (Psalm 139:17-18)

Do you hear that? Papa can't get you out of His mind! Shall we ask Him what He's been thinking? (Just relax and give yourself permission to write the first thing you sense Him saying.)

What was the first thought You had about me today when I woke up?

_____

_____

_____

What are Your favorite things about me?

_____

_____

_____

What do I do that makes You smile?

_____

_____

_____

What is most *true* about me that I have yet to believe?

_____

_____

_____

When you hear what He's thinking, amazing things happen! You begin to look just like His Son. It happens to you and for you, and the best part is that you don't have to do a thing but agree with Him. That's what we call an easy-breezy transformation!

Day Three

The wounds you receive on your journey through life have a way of seeping into your soul and distorting your identity. It twists how you see yourself and how you believe others see you. Before you know it, your life is far short of "adventurously expectant."

We've got great news for you! When you receive His Truth, your life becomes the living expression of God Himself who has made His home within you. So what is the remedy for relief from a distorted identity?

We overturn lies about our identity through the 3 R's:

> Release forgiveness
> Renounce lies
> Receive Truth

Write down one of your negative "I Am" statements from Day 1:

_____

_____

Ask Jesus to remind you when the first time that particular negative "I Am" statement was introduced to your life: (You may have a memory or an age that pops into your mind.)

_____

_____

Ask Jesus: Is there anyone I need to forgive for introducing this lie into my life?

Ask Jesus: How has believing this lie impacted my life?

(We call this your debt list - all the ways that this has cost you or impacted your life. Carrying this list is a heavy burden! But there's one person who is prepared to handle it for you and I bet you know His Name!)

Identify the debt list below:

What comes next is you being set free by releasing forgiveness as an expression of how deeply you have been forgiven. (Remember, this is for **you**. This doesn't say what they did to you was OK or justified in anyway. This is for your freedom, sister!)

Jesus, today I choose to forgive _____ for introducing this lie into my life. I place this debt list in your hands and release these debts to you. (See yourself handing it over to Him... what does He do with it?)

I declare this debt canceled in Jesus's mighty powerful, chain-breaking and freedom-giving name!

What do you see or sense?

Renounce the lie:

Jesus, today I renounce agreement with the lie that I am _____ !

I nail this lie to the cross and declare "**It** is finished!" Jesus, please come and wash every place that this lie has defiled my life, my emotions, my relationships, my thought life and my body! (Visualize this for added impact!)

Receive the Truth:

Jesus, what is the Truth that you give me in exchange for this lie?

_____

_____

Jesus, who do you say that I am?

_____

_____

Jesus, can you give me a picture of what my life would be like if I lived in agreement with this new "I am"?

_____

_____

How can you make the Truths He has just given you into declaration weapons to use in your life?

_____

_____

_____

_____

_____

_____

_____

_____

_____

_____

_____

When God changed Abram's name to Abraham, He wasn't just adding another syllable! He actually added the Hebrew letter "Hey" from **His Own Name** to Abraham's name.

The Hebrew language is so interesting in that the letters are both pictures and numbers. The picture for "Hey" is a man with His hands raised up in worship and means "to behold." It is also the number 5 which biblically is the number for "Grace." In other words, God's grace changed not only Abraham's name, but also his identity - he became someone to behold!

Did you know that when God's Grace came into your life, **YOU** got an upgrade? You became a woman of great grace that is someone to behold! In fact, you carry the very DNA of Jesus through your union with Him.

What are some declarations that you can make over your life that reflect your partnership with this new DNA of His amazing Grace?

_____

_____

_____

Who does *Grace* say you are now? Make it a declaration!

_____

_____

_____

What does *Grace* say you can do now? Make it a declaration!

_____

_____

_____

Sweet girl,

Turn around and let Me remove the labels that limit you. The truth of who you are is not found in your genes, your family, your title, your past, your marital status or your appearance. When you placed your faith in My son, you were grafted into My family. I am the God who makes all things new. Because of your faith in My Son, I have made you a new creation. You are in Christ and He is in You. Before the Cross, no one had ever known such a creation. Did you know that even Adam and Eve did not enjoy what you now have?

I have given you a new name to reflect your position as My daughter. I long for you to hear and embrace it. It is the identity I have bestowed on you that no circumstance can shake and nothing and no one can change. Your new name is not anything you can earn or lose. It's a reflection of who I am. My new name for you is a bold declaration of freedom from your past and hope for your future.

The journey of becoming your truest self begins by believing who I say you are. Your name tells the story of My great love and plans for you. Saturate yourself in the language of My love. Meditate day and night on who I say you are and whose you are. For I am the name above all names. All other names and labels must bow to My I Am! I created you. I chose you. You are My masterpiece. I call you: My Daughter, Accepted, Adopted, Blessed, Chosen, Co-laborer, Favored, Heir, Beloved, Righteous, Forgiven, Seen Known, Pure, Innocent, Beautiful, Wonderfully Made, Enough, Bride, New Creation, Strong, Whole, Clean, Free, Truth-Teller, Image-Bearer, More than a Conqueror, Overcomer, Radiant, Protected and Victorious. What if today were the day that you began to believe all that I say that you now are?

Love,
Abba Daddy

Beliefs for My Blueprint

What key phrases are Abba highlighting to you in the passages below? Underline or highlight them.

—— 1 JOHN 4:17 TPT
...because all that Jesus now is, so are we in this world.

—— PROVERBS 18:21 MSG
Words kill, words give life; they're either poison or fruit - you choose.

——EPHESIANS 1:4 TPT
And He chose us to be His very own, joining us to himself even before He laid the foundation of the universe! Because of His great love, He ordained us, so that we would be seen as holy in His eyes with an unstained innocence.

—— COLOSSIANS 2:9-14 TPT
For He is the complete fullness of deity living in human form. And our own completeness is not found in Him. We are completely filled with God as Christ's fullness overflows within us... Everything we once were in Adam has been placed onto His cross and nailed permanently there as a public display of cancellation.

—— 2 CORINTHIANS 5:17 NIV
Therefore, if anyone is in Christ, the new creation has come; The old has gone, the new is here!

—— EPHESIANS 2:10 TPT
We have become His poetry, a re-created people that will fulfill the destiny He has given each of us, for we are joined to Jesus, the Anointed One. Even before we were born, God planned in advance our destiny and the good works we would do to fulfill it!

—— EPHESIANS 1:3-4 NIV
Praise be to the God and Father of our Lord Jesus Christ, who has blessed us in the heavenly realms with every spiritual blessing in Christ. For He chose in Him before the creation of the world to be holy and blameless in His sight.

NOTES

"WALKING IN HIS FREEDOM AND
OVERWHELMING GOODNESS IS
GOING TO TAKE PRACTICE FOR
ME, BUT THE FLOODGATES ARE
BEGINNING TO OPEN. I WANT
TO SOAK IN THIS!"

♥ *Kathryn*

SESSION SEVEN
Who's Your Daddy

GOD DECIDED IN ADVANCE TO
ADOPT US INTO HIS OWN FAMILY
BY BRINGING US TO HIMSELF
THROUGH JESUS CHRIST. THIS IS
WHAT HE WANTED TO DO AND IT
GAVE HIM GREAT PLEASURE.

EPHESIANS 1:5 NLT

Somehow, the message of the Gospel has been distorted.

We have made it a message that we are sinners who need saving, and yet while that is entirely true, it is simply not the whole story. Jesus's gospel was that you are an orphan who needs a Father. In fact, the heartbeat of your good Father and the plan that has been in place since the beginning of time was for Jesus to bring you home to the Father so that He can love on you for all of eternity. At the cross, Jesus dealt with sin by completely removing it as an obstacle from the pathway home!

Before Jesus came, God was not known as Father. In fact, no one would have dared to call the God of the universe "Abba" or "Papa." We forget how truly revolutionary it was when Jesus taught His disciples to pray in what we refer to as the Lord's prayer. He told them when they prayed that they should approach God as their very own Heavenly Daddy, not just His Father! An exciting new chapter of relationship with the God of the universe was being unveiled before their very eyes.

Someone once said that the most important thing about you is what you believe about Father God. So, who do you say your Father is? In order to yield complete control of your life to Him, it will take believing in His uncompromised goodness, love and faithfulness to you as His child. Since Father God created you, He alone knows your "who" and "why" - who you are and why you are here. Apart from knowing your Heavenly Father, you will miss the who and why question every time! You will end up looking to people, relationships, possessions or careers to answer those questions.

Just like an orphan who gets adopted and has to get to know her new family, you too are on a journey of discovering who your real Heavenly Papa is. You may have your "forever papers" with your "forever home", but who is this forever Papa? Because our understanding is limited by what we are taught about our Heavenly Father or what we have gleaned from those around us coupled with the messages from culture and media, we tend to carry our Heavenly Father in a box of our own limited understanding. With a lifetime of influence, it's next to impossible to not have some distortion about who your Heavenly Father really is! Unfortunately, this Father we carry in our "boxes" rarely resembles Jesus's Papa.

If you had an emotionally absent father you may assume your Heavenly Father is distant also. If your own father was a heavy disciplinarian or had high performance standards, perhaps you view your Heavenly Father as strict, punitive or having unrealistic expectations.

On top of that, you may have grown up with a mixed religious view that pictures Jesus and Father God in different lights. Have you ever noticed how Jesus is usually cast as the "nice guy" of the Trinity while Father God is seen as the "angry judge"? And to some, Father God can be a lot like Santa, rewarding the "nice" but withholding from the "naughty." Whatever your concept of Father God is, we believe that you are in this study because Father God is ready to align your heart with the Truth that will set you free - the Truth as revealed in the Word of God and the person of Jesus!

The good news is Father understood just how misunderstood He truly was! So, He sent Jesus to take the lid off our boxes and to represent Him in the only way a true Son ever could; a Son who is the mirror image of His Father. If it were not for this profound statement, we might still be toting around our God in a box.

"If you have seen Him, you have seen the Father."
[JOHN 14:9]

LIKE WE HAD NEVER SEEN BEFORE

In other words, Jesus is the most perfect portrait the world has ever seen of what your Heavenly Father looks like. In modern terms, Jesus is God's selfie! When He stepped into history, your precious Father finally took center stage. It took Jesus coming full of "Grace and Truth" and getting up close and personal with humanity for you to truly grasp who your Heavenly Father is and to reconcile your understanding of what you believe about your Father. In short, if you don't see it in Jesus, it's not true of our Heavenly Father.

Listening Guide

[KEY #7]

I HAVE A GOOD FATHER WHO CALLS ME HIS BELOVED DAUGHTER.

Adam and Eve didn't just become sinners... they became _____ . Orphans can only guess what a Father is like - it takes a Son to tell you what He is really like! Jesus came and took the lid off our boxes.

"WHAT COMES INTO YOUR MIND WHEN YOU THINK ABOUT GOD IS THE MOST IMPORTANT THING ABOUT YOU" - AW TOZER

Ask Holy Spirit: Who is the Father that lives in my box? How do I picture Him?

_____

_____

_____

4 Myths that Undermine Our Faith in Father's Goodness:

Myth #1   Father God is like my earthly father.

_____

_____

_____

Myth #2   Father God causes pain to build character. (Romans 8:28)
                 *The father of lies attacks **you** because it hurts the heart of your Dad.*

_____

Myth #3   Father God is punishing the world to get people to repent.
               (John 3:16-17, Romans 2:4)
               Father God uses His kindness to get people to repent! ALL sins for ALL
               people for ALL time was paid at the cross.

_____

_____

Myth #4   Father God turns His back on me "in my hour of greatest need."
               (Psalm 22:24 TPT)

_____

_____

_____

What is our Father like? (Colossians 1:15, Hebrews 1:3)

_____

_____

_____

_____

Jesus is the **divine portrait** and the **exact expression** of God's true nature!

_____

_____

_____

_____

_____

_____

_____

_____

_____

Journal

Write down any impressions, pictures or feelings you experienced during the activation exercise. Ask Papa the following, "Papa, what are you saying to me?"

Daily Reflections

"JESUS IS THE PERFECT PORTRAIT OF WHAT
YOUR PAPA LOOKS LIKE."

Day One

Please review your session notes. What is Father God highlighting for you?

_____

_____

_____

What are your thoughts regarding this statement made by Karen, "I don't think we can become all we were intended to be as daughters until we know who our Heavenly Father truly is."

_____

_____

_____

Up until now, who is the Father that has lived in your box? What words or pictures come to mind?

_____

_____

_____

_____

What does Father God sound like? What tone does He take with you?

Did you identify with any of the 4 myths? What challenges did you encounter?

In what ways does your picture of Jesus and Father God differ?

Write a prayer below to ask for help in wrestling through some of what has come up for you. And remember, "The spirit of adoption is at work to make God's fatherhood real to you."

Day Two

The Spirit you received does not make you slaves, so that you live in
fear again; rather, the Spirit you received brought about your adoption
to sonship. And by Him we cry, Abba, Father.
[ROMANS 8:15]

You are on a journey to discover how magnificent your Heavenly Papa truly is - Holy Spirit is ready to take the lid off your box! Religious teachings and the environment you grew up in can both contribute to a view of your Father that is, well, twisted! Your relationship with your own earthly father - or lack of relationship as is the case with death, emotional absence or divorce/abandonment - can certainly influence your beliefs. Today is the day to align your heart with who He really is: a good Father who will never leave you or hurt you. He's a Father who adores you and cares about even the smallest details of your life!

Complete the following exercise to see how your views might be influenced.

Place an X along the continuum to describe how you see Father God.
Place an * along the continuum to describe how you see/saw your own earthly father or father figure.

PATIENT	IMPATIENT
KIND	HARSH
LOVING	ANGRY
FORGIVING	PUNITIVE
WARM	COLD
PRESENT	ABSENT
APPROACHABLE	DISTANT
GENEROUS	STINGY
FAITHFUL	UNPREDICTABLE
INVOLVED	UNINVOLVED

If the way you view your Heavenly Father doesn't line up with the descriptive words on the left side of the chart, then you are being invited to "upgrade" your view of Him! However, in order to have a new view of your Heavenly Father, you may need to forgive your earthly father (or other male figures) for how he misrepresented your Heavenly Father.

This can sometimes be a painful process as we acknowledge how our own fathers may not have met our needs well or may have misrepresented how truly perfect Papa is. Here's where it is helpful to remember that your earthly father grew up in an imperfect world with his own wounds, flesh patterns and lies. Bottom line: this is not about blaming them but healing you!

Use this prayer to guide you in releasing forgiveness. Fill in the blanks and speak them aloud.

Today I choose to forgive _____ for _____

_____

When he did that, I felt _____

_____

When he did that, I believed _____

_____

The consequences/outcomes of these beliefs in my life are: _____

_____

_____

I can see now that it caused me to see you, Papa God, as _____ .

_____

Today I chose to release all of this to you Papa.

Imagine placing your earthly father at the foot of the cross and entrusting him to Jesus. Invite Papa to take your hand as you turn to walk away and head back to His House.

Now climb up in His lap in His big chair and tell Him what you need from Him. Lay it all out.

Do you need to be able to trust Him? To know He will provide for you and not hurt you?
Do you need to know that He has a plan for your life and that you are going to be alright?

As you share your heart, pause and listen. What is His response to you? Don't edit! Just write!

What insights do you gain from this exercise?

Day Three

Everywhere Jesus went we encounter His immeasurable goodness - healing ALL who came to Him, delivering people from demonic torment, raising the dead, forgiving sinners, loving the unlovely and dining with the disreputable. On His last day on earth, He makes this bombshell statement that is meant to echo in our hearts still today.

"Jesus answered... Anyone who has seen me has seen the Father." (John 14:9 NIV)

If Jesus is just like the Father in every way, what do you think Jesus is trying to change when it comes to your thoughts regarding your Heavenly Father?

_____

_____

_____

Read Luke 15:11-32.
In the prodigal son story, Jesus was painting a portrait of what his very own Father was like! Take a few moments and imagine yourself in this story.

What does Jesus want you to see about the Father? What desires do you experience as you now contemplate who Papa is?

_____

_____

_____

Now, let's do some freestyle journaling. Fill in the following as Holy Spirit leads you.

Dear Beloved Daughter,

I am so pleased that you _____

I have been waiting for you to _____

You have been mistaken when you thought that I was _____

I can't wait for you to _____

What do you want to declare over your life this week? Here are some ideas to get you started. What would you like to add?

I am chosen, adopted and a beloved daughter of the Most High who happens to be my Father! I belong to the greatest family on earth. I have the privilege of calling you _____ .
I trust my Heavenly Father to reveal to me who I am and why I am here. You are good and only do good. I know the Truth and the Truth sets me free. Jesus is just like my Daddy - there's no one quite like Him!

Day Five

My beloved daughter,

I deeply love your earthly father, yet in his humanness, he simply was unable to love and bless you with everything you need as a daughter. So today, I want to give you My perfect blessing. I want you to receive, at the deepest level of your being, the gift of My heart for you as your Good Father.

I call your spirit to life as My daughter. I call you to rise up with renewed strength under the shelter of My love. I call every part of your body, soul and spirit to recognize your identity as My child. There is no confusion in you; you are blessed to be My daughter.

I bless the day I chose you before the foundation of the world. There has never been a day I did not want you, love you or adore you.

I bless the day I knit you together in your mother's womb. I took such care to intricately craft you and design you to so perfectly reflect My image. I bless every cell of your body with acceptance, sustenance, healing, strength and energy.

I bless your soul. The lies that have shackled you are powerless when you see what I see when I look at you! Every wound inflicted upon your precious heart will find full restoration as you lean into my perfect love. I release you from thinking you are a burden, too much, not enough, rejected or abandoned. I bless your spirit and call it to full attention. You will live from this day forward knowing that I bestow upon you full power and authority.

I bless you to run into My arms with reckless abandon knowing I'll never let you fall. I bless you to know with full confidence that you are never alone. You are Mine. I bless you to know that We would have gone to the cross even if it was only just for you.

You are worth it. I see you. I know you. I free you today from the oppressing spirits that have tried to put you into bondage. They are powerless before Me. They must release you now in the name of My precious Son, Jesus.

I bless all of the days of your life to be saturated with My love and Grace. I bless you to live an adventurously expectant life full of My joy. And with this my daughter... nothing can stop you from coming fully alive as the daughter you are and the daughter I call you to be.

Love,
Papa

Beliefs for My Blueprint

What key phrases are Abba highlighting to you in the passages below? Underline or highlight them.

—— EPHESIANS 1:5-6 TPT
For it was always in his perfect plan to adopt us as his delightful children, through our union with Jesus, the Anointed One, so that his tremendous love that cascades over us would glorify his grace —for the same love he has for the Beloved, Jesus, he has for us. And this unfolding plan brings him great pleasure!

—— JOHN 14:9 NIV
... Anyone who has seen me has seen the Father... How could you ask me to show you the Father, for anyone who has looked at me has seen the Father. Don't you believe that the Father is living in me and that I am living in the Father? Even my words are not my own but come from my Father, for He lives in me...

——ROMANS 8:15-17 TPT
But you have received the "Spirit of full acceptance," enfolding you into the family of God. And you will never feel orphaned, for as He rises up within us, our spirits join Him in saying the words of tender affection, "Beloved Father!" For the Holy Spirit makes God's fatherhood real to us as He whispers into our innermost being, "You are God's beloved child!" And since we are His true children, we qualify to share all His treasures, for indeed, we are heirs of God himself. And since we are joined to Christ, we also inherit all that He is and all that He has.

—— PSALM 147:3 NIV
He heals the brokenhearted and binds up their wounds.

—— ROMANS 5:10 TPT
And because of the sacrifice of Jesus, you will never experience the wrath of God.

——I JOHN 3:1 TPT
Look with wonder at the depth of the Father's marvelous love that He has lavished on us! He has called us and made us His very own beloved children!

NOTES

"WHAT IF I HONESTLY BELIEVED

I AM WHO HE SAYS I AM? WHAT

IF I PERFORMED GREATER

MIRACLES THAN JESUS? WHAT

IF I CLAIMED HIS PROMISES

EACH DAY FOR ME AND FOR

THOSE HE PUTS IN MY PATH?"

♥ *Amanda*

SESSION EIGHT

There Is More

WHOEVER BELIEVES IN ME WILL

DO THE WORKS I HAVE BEEN

DOING, AND THEY WILL DO

EVEN GREATER THINGS THAN

THESE BECAUSE I AM GOING

TO THE FATHER.

———————

JOHN 14:12

The Gospel of Grace declares...

that as a daughter in your Father's House you are lavishly loved, fully forgiven and radically righteous. But the gift of Grace doesn't come close to stopping there. Let's take a look at the unfathomable promise Papa gives us in Ephesians 3:20, "He will achieve infinitely more than your greatest request, your most unbelievable dream and exceed your wildest imagination. He will outdo them all, for His miraculous power constantly energizes you."

Wow!!! We hope this study has opened your eyes and your heart to the Truth that in Him there is always MORE - more love, more joy, more abundance, more freedom and more power to experience. This session focuses on the fact that as daughters, we have the awesome responsibility to not only receive His Grace and love but to be a vessel that pours it out freely to others. We have been extended an invitation to partner with our Father to bring Heaven to earth and transform the culture of our families and communities, even as we have been transformed through His amazing Grace.

Life as a daughter in your Father's House has the potential to be the most exciting life you could ever live. Imagine walking a day in Jesus's shoes. Picture yourself along the shores of Galilee where He healed the leper. Or, put yourself in the village of Bethany when Lazarus came stumbling into the sunshine with grave clothes hanging off of him. Jesus was constantly breaking the glass ceiling on what people believed a mere man could do. We can easily dismiss His astounding works because He is the Son of God. We think, "Well of course He can do these miraculous things!"

But, ask yourself, who am I? You are the daughter of God! The same Spirit that moved so powerfully in Jesus is the same Spirit that longs to move powerfully in you. The promise Jesus made in John 14:12 is that if you believe in Him then you will do even greater things because He is going to prepare a place for you in Father's House. You've been given the permission and power to not only REPEAT what the Father says, but to DEMONSTRATE what He does! In fact, the Gospel is so much more than a story to be repeated - it is truly a "show and tell" Gospel!

As the Holy Spirit continues to make Himself even more real in your life, greater and more powerful things will happen in and through you. What an incredible opportunity we've been entrusted with. Let's not squander it by living inside the limits we've placed on ourselves and our Father. If He is in you, then so is His Kingdom realm! Stand on the feet of your Father and dance in His presence. Follow His lead to LIVE and DREAM BIG!

There's really only one thing standing between you and this adventurously expectant life! Are you thirsty? Holy Spirit is ready to pour into your life in greater measure. He delights when you ask Him for MORE!

Listening Guide

[KEY #8]

I BELIEVE I WAS MADE FOR MORE.

Father God wants you to become the "Go-To" gal for your family, friends and community!

A "Go-To" gal is a woman others go to because she knows who she is and who has her back - Papa and His extravagant, powerful Kingdom! She's a girl who has stepped out of her comfort zone, walks on the waters of Grace and experiences the "adventurously expectant" life!

Thirst and Humility are the _____ to becoming a Go-To Girl!

The enemy's goal is to keep you from discovering you were made for _____ .

So what should you know about the Holy Spirit?

 Holy Spirit has good gifts to give! (1 Corinthians 12:7-11)

_____

_____

_____

Holy Spirit is the _____ for God to fulfill His will in you and through you. God's will is... On earth as it is in heaven!

The Gospel is not just a message we repeat but a life we _____ .

_____

_____

Holy Spirit wants to release the _____ off of your life.

_____

_____

_____

Are you thirsty for MORE?

"Which of you fathers, if your son asks for a fish, will give him a snake instead? Or if He asks for an egg, will give him a scorpion. If you then, though you are evil, know how to give good gifts to your children, how much more will your Father in heaven give the Holy Spirit to those who ask him!" (Luke 11:11-13 NIV)

Journal

Write down any impressions, pictures or feelings you experienced during the activation exercise. ASK Papa the following, "Papa, what are you saying to me?"

_____

_____

_____

_____

_____

_____

_____

_____

_____

_____

_____

_____

Daily Reflections

Day One

Please review your session notes. What is Father God highlighting for you?

_____

_____

_____

Up until now, in what ways have you put a lid on the box of Holy Spirit?

_____

_____

_____

What challenges did you encounter as you heard today's message? What was new for you?

_____

_____

_____

_____

_____

The statement was made, "We have made the gospel about a story we REPEAT rather than a life we DEMONSTRATE." What might change in your life if you believed you could be a demonstrator of the Good News and not just a repeater?

_____

_____

_____

Read Luke 11:11-13. What do you want to ask for?

_____

_____

_____

Day Two

Do you remember Peter's denial and betrayal of Jesus and how terrified he was of being associated with Jesus? And yet just 50 days later, this same Peter stood up on the day of Pentecost and boldly preached a sermon by which 3,000 people put their faith in Jesus believing who He said He was - the Son of God who came to "sozo" the world!

What happened? Peter was filled to overflowing with Holy Spirit and simply spilled out everywhere he went! Guess what? So can you!

When you are filled with Holy Spirit, things change. You will discover a boldness in your life, an exhilarating freedom and the power to do things you couldn't do before. He's just that good and that exciting to do life with!

Read the following passages and record your observations about Holy Spirit and a life of "MORE."

John 7:37-39

_____

_____

_____

Acts 3:1-12

_____

_____

_____

Acts 19:1-6

_____

_____

_____

Acts 4:29-31

_____

_____

_____

Friend, it's time to do some daydreaming. If you truly believed Holy Spirit was this powerful in you... (remember as He is, so are you!)

What would you believe?

_____

_____

_____

What would you do?

_____

_____

_____

What would you ask for?

_____

_____

Spend a few moments in fellowship with Holy Spirit - thank Him for His presence in your life. Ask Him to fill you to overflowing and for your sensitivity to His gentle leadings be increased. Imagine an elevator dropping from your head (your mind) and down into your belly where scripture tells us living waters flow. Picture yielding yourself to Him... opening the doors of the elevator and allowing His life giving Spirit to fill you up!

What do you sense as you do this?

Let's begin by reading Luke 9:1-6 and Luke 10:1-9.

In the above passages, we see what life looks like when Holy Spirit moves powerfully in Papa's children. The amazing thing is that this happened before Holy Spirit was even poured out in full measure at Pentecost. What does that say to you and I who live on the other side of the Cross in Sunday's resurrection power?

I absolutely LOVE how Jesus sent them out without Him by their side. How much easier it would have been to think you could heal the sick if you had the Healer standing next to you? But Jesus was taking off the training wheels... just like He wants to do for you! They were being invited to step into a new kind of life... just like He is inviting you!! Here's the bottom line: They needed 2 things - the Holy Spirit and the belief that in the same way Papa sent Jesus, He was sending them!

What if you really believed that the same Holy Spirit wants to move powerfully for you? Perhaps you were placed in this Bible study to discover this one thing: you are a powerful daughter with a powerful Papa!

Let's practice

Choose one of the following stories:

- A woman delivered from a spirit of infirmity (Luke 13:10-13)
- Peter walks on water (Matt 14:22-33)
- Peter and John heal the lame man (Act 3:1-9)

Imagine yourself at the scene. Try to picture every detail. Where are you in the story? What is the environment like? What is the atmosphere/mood like?

Now see yourself stepping into the action, into your full power and authority as a daughter who is filled with the same Spirit who raised Jesus from the dead! See yourself believing that all of Heaven stands ready to back you up - just like Jesus - because you are ONE with Him!

What happens next? Journal any thoughts or impressions that come up for you.

_____

_____

_____

_____

_____

_____

_____

_____

_____

_____

Day Four

Please fill in the following with your name:

His kingdom come, His will be done on earth as it is in heaven through_____.
(Matthew 6:10)

_____ was anointed by God and with the Holy Spirit and with great power. She did wonderful things for others and divinely healed all who were under the tyranny of the devil, for God had anointed _____ . (Acts 10:38 TPT)

_____ , you shall do even greater things than I did because I am going to my Father. Whatever you ask Him in my name, I will do it. (John 14:12)

_____ , heal the sick, raise the dead, cleanse the lepers, drive out demons. Freely you have received, now freely give. (Matthew 10:8)

What would change in your life if you began to believe these verses were already true of you?

_____

_____

_____

My beloved daughter,

Oh, how I've loved this journey with you. It's been such a joy to see your heart expand with the awareness of My goodness and My love for you. Do you see how simple it really is to live as a powerful daughter? All you need is to recognize your thirst and then simply ask Me to fill you. And daughter, Holy Spirit will pour rivers into you and out of you! I simply love blessing your desire.

The plans We have been dreaming over you are more than your wildest imagination. In the days to come We will make that beautiful imagination come alive to the more that We have for you. Indeed, We are anointing you on this journey with resurrection power! You have My authority to bring the kingdom of Heaven to earth. I commission you to change the atmosphere of every environment you enter with My love, My Grace and My freedom. I grant you the keys of My kingdom to unleash peace, joy, hope and love to those with whom you interact.

I bless you to continue walking out this journey with bold confidence in the freedom of knowing who you are as My daughter. Whenever you feel lost, seek My voice - pause and listen. We are right there! Whenever you feel weary, rest in My embrace. Whenever you feel alone, remember My comforter resides within you. Whenever you feel defeated, know the victory has already been won. You are precious beyond words. I will never leave you nor forsake you - it's just not part of My vocabulary, beloved one. I'm so proud of you... My lavishly loved, fully forgiven and radically righteous daughter!

Love, *Papa*

Beliefs for My Blueprint

What key phrases are Abba highlighting to you in the passages below? Underline or highlight them.

—— ACTS 10:38 NIV
How God anointed Jesus of Nazareth with the Holy Spirit and power, and how He went around doing good and healing all who were under the power of the devil, because God was with Him.

—— LUKE 10:8 TPT
When you enter into a new town, and you have been welcomed by its people, follow these rules: Eat what is served you. Then heal the sick, and tell them all, "God's kingdom realm has arrived and is now within your reach!"

——1 CORINTHIANS 12:13 NIV
For we were all baptized by one Spirit so as to form one body - whether Jews or Gentiles, slave or free - and we were all given the one Spirit to drink.

—— JOHN 14:12 NIV
Whoever believes in me will do the works I have been doing, and they will do even greater things than these because I am going to the Father.

—— MATTHEW 6:10 NIV
Your kingdom come, your will be done on earth as it is in heaven.

—— LUKE 11:11-13 NIV
Which of you fathers, if your son asks for a fish, will give him a snake instead? Or if he asks for an egg, will give him a scorpion? If you then, though you are evil, know how to give good gifts to your children, how much more will your Father in heaven give the Holy Spirit to those who ask Him?

Suggested Listening

WEEK 1
Waymaker, Leeland
Running in Circles, United Pursuit

WEEK 2
Jesus Loves Me, Tomlin
I am Loved, Maverick City Music

WEEK 3
Living Hope, Bethel Music
Clean, Natalie Grant
Mistakes, Influence Music

WEEK 4
No Longer Slaves, Bethel Music
Death Was Arrested Live, NorthPoint Music
Run to the Father, Cody Carnes

WEEK 5
The Blessing, Kari Jobe/Cody Carnes
New Wine, Hillsong

WEEK 6
Sons and Daughters, NorthPoint Worship
Who You Say I Am, Hillsong
I Know You, Bellarive

WEEK 7
Wide Open, Clay Finnesand
The Father's House, Cory Asbury
You Never Let Go, Torwalt

WEEK 8
Goodness of God, Bethel
Tremble/What a Beautiful Name, Phil Wickham
Set a Fire, United Pursuit
In Over My Head, Bethel

Answer Key

Father God loves me as much as He loves Jesus.   **TRUE**
(Session 2 - Romans 5:8, John 3:16, Ephesians 3:19, Romans 8:38-39)

Papa's love for you is unlimited, unconditional and so extravagant that He was willing to give His own son's life to demonstrate this lavish love. In Ephesians 3:19, Paul even prays that we would have a revelation of this love that actually surpasses knowledge or human understanding. When we doubt His love, we can remind ourselves that Father God loves Jesus and Father God placed Christ in us so that every question about His love for us would be settled.

Fellowship with Father God is broken until I confess and repent.   **FALSE**
(Session 3 - Colossians 2:13-15, Colossians 1:22, Hebrews 10:17, Romans 8:1, Matthew 26:28)

Once you are IN Christ, fellowship with Father God is never broken, even if you sin. Why? Because Jesus was and still is the perfect solution and answer to the horrible "broken fellowship" problem that we ALL had as a result of the fall. Your new spirit is holy, innocent and righteous before the Lord. This belief that fellowship is broken until I do something to restore the relationship is actually a holdover of the Old Covenant (Is 59:2), but it is not the New Covenant. In fact, the word repent actually means to change your mind - it's not what YOU do to change GOD'S mind about you. In the New Covenant, Father God relates to you on the basis of "It is finished." The blood of Jesus paid your sin-debt in full for all time so that if you sin you can run to Father God and experience the joy of relationship! Your sins have been cast into the sea and are remembered no more!

God answers my prayers on the basis of my obedience to Him.   **FALSE**
(Session 4 - James 5:16, Mark 11:24, Matthew 7:11)

Father God answers my prayers on the basis of my position as a daughter seated next to Him in heavenly places, not on the basis of my performance or obedience. This is the amazing nature of Grace! This belief is another holdover of the Old Covenant - if I obey, then God will bless me (Deuteronomy 28). Under the New Covenant, God answers your prayers on the basis of your position. In fact, as a good Father, He actually loves to answer your prayers, to bless you, to guide you and to open doors of opportunity in your life - not as a reward, but simply because you are a daughter who has an incredible inheritance and has been fully qualified for every blessing.

I am as righteous as Jesus Christ. TRUE
(Session 4 - Romans 5:1-2, 2 Corinthians 5:21, Romans 5:15-16)

We have been given the righteousness of God in Christ Jesus. You are as righteous as Jesus because He gave you His very own righteousness. We cannot earn, merit, qualify or achieve this righteousness. It is simply given to us as a free gift, and it is received by faith. Righteousness is our new position before God and describes our new identity. In the same way that there's nothing you can do to add to your righteousness, there's nothing you can do to take away from it. Why? Because it is within Jesus's rights and perfect will to give you all that He is - perfect righteousness!

I should work hard to live according to the Ten Commandments. FALSE
(Session 5 - Romans 5:20, Galatians 3:23-25, Matthew 5:17, Romans 7:7, Romans 3:19-21, 2 Corinthians 3:6, James 2:10)

Life in the New Covenant is an entirely different kind of life that is lived from an entirely different source. Under the Old Covenant, followers of God did not have the Holy Spirit to lead them, much less energize them with new life. Under the Old Covenant, life was defined by self-effort and striving to live up to the Ten Commandments. These commandments reveal God's holiness, but they cannot make us holy. In the New Covenant we begin from a place of trust that Jesus fulfilled the Law on our behalf! We don't live according to the rules but from relationship with God. Thus, we are re-birthed into a new life! We are now led by the Spirit of God into a life that is pleasing to Him as we simply yield to the leading of the Spirit of Life within us. Following His leading leads us in the ways of righteousness and teaches us to say no to all ungodliness.

My righteousness before God is dependent on whether I am living right before God. FALSE
(Session 4 - 2 Corinthians 5:21, Romans 5:17-21)

This is truly the scandal of Grace! This position of righteousness does not fluctuate with your performance, obedience or behavior. Christ's righteousness is your new identity - your new position before the Father. What happens if you don't "live right"? Does that change your righteousness? No. Because it is not your righteousness. You've been given Christ's unchanging righteousness.

The Holy Spirit's primary role is to convict me of sin. FALSE
(Session 3 - John 16:13, John 16:8-11, Romans 8:1-2, Galatians 4:6)

Unfortunately, most believers have been taught that the most important and primary role of the Holy Spirit is to tell them every time they sin. This is simply not the way the Kingdom works. Does He want to keep you from hurting yourself and hurting other? Absolutely. He never condemns, but He will correct us for our good. However, Holy Spirit has many other roles as well. He is there to instruct you, to lead you, to comfort you, to nurture you and to lead you into all Truth. He leads you into freedom, joy and peace and reveals the Kingdom in you. He reveals your true identity as a daughter of God and convinces you of your new righteous position. He has been given to reveal to you that there is now no condemnation for you... not ever. Instead, He reminds you of who you are - Forgiven, Innocent and as Righteous as Jesus.

Everything that Jesus said applies to my life.   **FALSE**
(Session 5)

The Gospels reflect a period of transition from Law to Grace and Old to New. This is why context is so key. Some things Jesus said were spoken specifically for His audience - people who were living under the Old Covenant. As a New Covenant believer, you are not under the Law/Old Covenant (in fact, it was never your covenant). If we read the red letters of Jesus and try to apply everything Jesus said to our life, we can end up confused (am I forgiven or not?), hurt (cut an arm off or pluck out an eye) and even hopeless. It is imperative that you rightly divide the Word by asking the questions: WHO is the audience and WHAT is the purpose for what He is saying?

My identity is a sinner who is saved by Grace.   **FALSE**
(Session 6 - Colossians 1:2, 2 Corinthians 5:17, 1 John 4:17, Colossians 2:9-14, Romans 8:1)

You were a sinner, but that is no longer who you are! You got a complete identity change when you put your faith in Christ. The old you - sinner - died with Christ. You were resurrected with Him in Christ and are now a saint! Even if you sin, your actions cannot undo what Christ has done when He recreated you and made you new! Grace says you are righteous! You are a daughter! You are innocent!

God will sometimes cause accidents or sickness to grow people in their faith or test them.
(Session 7 - Jeremiah 32:40, John 10:10, Isaiah 53:4-5, Isaiah 54:9-10)   **FALSE**

As a New Covenant believer, you are promised that God will never leave you, never punish you and never be angry with you. You are promised that He will be faithful to you, protect you, love you and forgive you. He will uphold you, heal you and never cease doing good to you. The important distinction here is who we attribute blame to for our suffering. God is not the originator of your pain. God is good! He would never cause harm to you through sickness or accidents because it would be inconsistent with the nature of who He is and what He says you have in this amazing New Covenant of Grace. Don't fall for the scheme of the enemy who wants to blame Papa God for his own evil actions.

Made in the USA
Columbia, SC
08 September 2023

22613974R00089